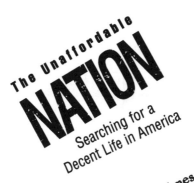

The Unaffordable NATION

Searching for a Decent Life in America

Jeffrey D. Jones

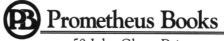 **Prometheus Books**

59 John Glenn Drive
Amherst, New York 14228-2197

Published 2007 by Prometheus Books

Inquiries should be addressed to
Prometheus Books
59 John Glenn Drive
Amherst, New York 14228–2197
VOICE: 716–691–0133, ext. 210
FAX: 716–691–0137
WWW.PROMETHEUSBOOKS.COM

11 10 09 08 07   5 4 3 2 1

Library of Congress Cataloging-in-Publication Data

Jones, Jeffrey.
    The unaffordable nation : searching for a decent life in America / Jeffrey Jones
        p. cm.
    Includes bibliographical references and index.
    ISBN 978–1–59102–515–3 (alk. paper)
    1. Cost and standard of living—United States. 2. Public welfare—United States.
3. United States—Social policy—1993– I. Title.
HD6983.J66 2007
339.4'20973—dc22

                                                                2007001564

Printed in the United States on acid-free paper

Contents

ACKNOWLEDGMENTS 7

FOREWORD BY STEPHEN NATHANSON 11

INTRODUCTION: LEIBNIZ IN ECONOMICS 17

PART 1: THE UNAFFORDABLE NATION 33

Introduction: Products, Persons, and Unaffordability 35

Chapter 1: Of Lawsuits and Lotteries 41

Chapter 2: Traditionalism and the Rise of the
Credit Welfare System 57

Chapter 3: An Examination of a Noble Sentiment 75

Chapter 4: The Billionaire and the Destitute Man:
Unaffordability as a Political Problem 85

PART 2: POOR CHOICE, POOR JUSTICE, POOR LUCK   97

Introduction: Labor Obligations and Excuses   97

Chapter 5:   Poor Choice: The American Hatred of Paupers   103

Chapter 6:   Poor Justice: Injustice and the Golden Rule   123

Chapter 7:   Poor Luck: The Inequity of Disability
             and Other Struggles   133

PART 3: THE COVENANT ON AFFORDABILITY   143

Introduction: Labor-Based Entitlements   143

Chapter 8:   The Covenant on Affordability   147

Chapter 9:   Some Applications:
             Corporations, Immigration, and Trade   157

CONCLUSION: LABOR AS AN AMERICAN INSTITUTION   179

BIBLIOGRAPHY   189

INDEX   193

Acknowledgments

I began taking notes for what would become *The Unaffordable Nation* in the academic year of 2000 to 2001. I spent that year as a postdoctoral scholar in Glenn Loury's Institute on Race and Social Division at Boston University, and away from my position as an assistant professor of philosophy at the University of Massachusetts–Boston.

Truly, I intended to spend the IRSD year pursuing some race-related issues that grew out of my dissertation, a rather flawed work on citizenship and civic education. Fortunately, or unfortunately, the intense interdisciplinary discussions between legal scholars, philosophers, economists, political scientists, sociologists, and others that took place in the IRSD that year carried my research interests in entirely new directions.

In particular, the IRSD weekly seminars and discussions created a special interest in the ways that Americans think about work: how it is institutionalized through American law, turned politically toward goals such as efficiency or justice, the social functions it performs in addition to commercial production, and its vulnerability to internal forces such as social attitudes about economic freedom and external forces such as economic globalism.

Ultimately, Glenn provided invaluable comments on the book's conceptual approach. Indeed, the brief conversations I had with him about the project uncovered issues and implications I hadn't even thought of. But long before that, some of Glenn's observations concerning the limitations of analytic philosophy in public debate convinced me that, if possible, *The Unaffordable Nation* should in a manner be accessible to a nonacademic audience.

7

Thanks to David Lyons, my IRSD year doubled as a year as a visiting scholar at Boston University's School of Law. The access to the law school, the law faculty workshops, and the law courses helped me lay the foundation of an intellectual framework for pursuing the newfound interest in the morality of labor. The time spent at Boston University's School of Law also convinced me to seek a law degree. David read the first draft of several chapters of the manuscript and registered his objections, which were taken to heart.

I continued to tinker with the project over three years at the University of Michigan Law School. Unbeknownst to her, while at Michigan I received a lot of help on the project from Elizabeth Anderson, for whom I served multiple times as a teaching assistant in her law and philosophy course. I found Elizabeth's own philosophical writings on economics and racial integration extremely valuable. Elizabeth read some or all of a later draft of the manuscript and provided me with some excellent suggestions.

During my time at Michigan, I was also influenced by Thomas Green's forthcoming work, *Freedom and Criminal Responsibility in American Legal Thought* (New York: Cambridge University Press), for which I conducted some minor research. Early parts of his manuscript and several of his articles informed my treatment of Americans' attitudes toward work, their presumption of the freedom of individuals to earn everything they need to live decently, and the role that this presumption plays in the American understanding of work-related disability.

Parts of the book have much deeper roots. Lawrence Blum, my friend, colleague, and mentor at the University of Massachusetts–Boston, undertook a careful review of the entire manuscript. Among other things, his observations convinced me that one chapter was untenable and that another needed adding. The final product also makes good use of many sources that he recommended. Even before this project, however, Blum, Larry Foster, and the entire University of Massachusetts–Boston faculty had made substantial personal and institutional investments in me, for which I am forever grateful.

I am similarly indebted to the Department of Philosophy at the University of Wisconsin–Madison, in particular to Michael Byrd, Harry Brighouse, Patrick Riley, Francis Schrag, and Marcus Singer. From Wisconsin, special thanks are due to Lester Hunt and Ajume Wingo. Almost single-handedly, Lester taught me political philosophy from my freshman undergraduate year to completion of my doctoral degree. Ajume has been a steadfast friend and role model for nearly as long, in whose footsteps I continue to follow.

Thanks, finally, to Stephen Nathanson for writing the foreword to the book. His small book *Economic Justice* was an important source of inspiration for *The Unaffordable Nation*.

Foreword

By Stephen Nathanson

In the 1960s, President Lyndon Johnson declared a "War on Poverty." Like Johnson's war in Vietnam, his war on poverty is widely viewed as a failure. Poverty, after all, still exists in the United States. But in fact, during the Johnson years and through the 1970s, poverty rates in the United States went down. They took a turn upward in the 1980s when the Reagan administration changed tax codes and promoted cutbacks on "welfare spending." In fact, spending on poverty relief was viewed so negatively by so many Americans that a Democratic president, Bill Clinton, adopted the aim of "ending welfare as we know it."

If welfare spending was targeted at alleviating poverty, why did a Democratic president want to curtail or end it? Clinton aimed to alter welfare programs because they were perceived as undeserved handouts to people who were too lazy to work. In place of welfare "as we knew it," Clinton sought to create programs that would enable people to move into the workforce and become self-sufficient.

Although Jeffrey Jones does not discuss this particular development in *The Unaffordable Nation*, much of this book deals with the hostility toward the poor that runs through American culture and its roots in the cultural norms that make up the American work ethic. As Jones shows, the American work ethic makes heavy demands on individuals but lacks a corresponding set of obligations for employers. While people are expected to work for a living, there is no parallel demand that employers pay a living wage.

The Unaffordable Nation explores and analyzes the American work ethic and shows that it is not working. The main reason it is not working is that many Americans who work full-time do not earn enough to be able afford what is necessary for a decent life in our society.

This central fact about American life is related to the failures of both the War on Poverty and the Clinton welfare reforms. Both of these programs rested on the assumption that jobs are the solution to poverty. This analysis is flawed for two reasons. The first is that many people in poverty cannot work: they are children, elderly, disabled, or physically or mentally ill. All of these are large groups who cannot be expected to work full-time. The second problem with the assumption that jobs are the cure for poverty is that many poor people do work. They simply don't earn enough. This is the central fact that *The Unaffordable Nation* deals with: the mismatch between the amount of money that many jobs pay and the amount that people need to afford a decent life in America. As the book makes clear, this mismatch shows itself in the passion for lotteries among the poor, the increase in lawsuits, and the rise in credit card debt. The first two are strategies for striking it rich, while the second is a strategy for closing the gap between people's earnings and what is required for a decent life in America.

One way to describe the root problem is to see that the American work ethic rests on three beliefs that don't fit together coherently. The first is that people should work in order to take care of themselves. The second is that work should provide an income that is adequate for a decent life. The third is that a free market economy will provide people with both jobs and adequate pay. The harsh reality is that in a pure market economy, wages, like everything else, are largely determined by supply and demand, not by the needs of workers and their families. Where the supply of labor is larger than the demand, wages will go down. While wages are set by market forces, the amount needed for a decent life is set by quite different factors, including the biological needs that must be met if people are to survive and the social norms that determine what counts as a decent life. There is no guarantee that a market process of wage setting will yield a living wage for workers.

This is not a new problem. Adam Smith discussed it in the eighteenth century, and it occupied the thinking of the great nineteenth-century economic theorists Thomas Malthus, David Ricardo, John Stuart Mill, and Karl Marx. Nonetheless, it is a problem that our national mythology encourages us to ignore.

Why might the labor supply exceed the demand for laborers and thus bring down wage levels? One is population growth, which results from both longer life spans and lower mortality rates for infants and children. A second reason has to do with technological advances. New machinery can get work done with fewer human laborers. Earth-moving machinery replaces men with picks and shovels. Robots replace laborers on auto assembly lines. Desktop computers and printers replace typesetters. ATM machines replace bank tellers. At the same time, globalization and improved communications expand the labor pool to include people beyond national borders. These impersonal processes proceed without concern for their impact on the prospects for workers, and together they create downward pressures on wages.

These facts about the determinants of wages have been known for hundreds of years, and yet within our American cultural understanding, poverty is blamed on individuals. The myth persists that individual effort and individual motivation determine success and failure. As long as this myth is accepted, the poor will be seen as deserving their poverty. For those of us who are not poor, this is a comforting belief. If a person's being poor is his or her own fault, then it is not an injustice, and the rest of us have no duty to alleviate or abolish poverty. Poverty is simply what some people deserve for their voluntary inactivity.

In *The Unaffordable Nation,* Jones explores many aspects of these important issues and defends the need for social and political intervention to make sure that Americans who work can afford a decent life. If the message of the book were widely absorbed, the promise that American society implicitly makes to its members might actually be fulfilled. Until then, we will continue to adopt harsh policies that rest on implausible myths. At the same time, our national mythology will allow us to continue feeling proud that our country succeeds in providing "liberty and justice for all."

Some of you, we all know, are poor, find it hard to live, are sometimes, as it were, gasping for breath. I have no doubt that some of you who read this book are unable to pay for all the dinners which you have actually eaten, or for the coats and shoes which are fast wearing or are already worn out, and have come to this page to spend borrowed or stolen time, robbing your creditors of an hour. It is very evident what mean and sneaking lives many of you live, for my sight has been whetted by experience; always on the limits, trying to get into business and out of debt, a very ancient slough, called by the Latins aes alienum, *another's brass, for some of their coins were made of brass; still living, and dying, and buried by this other's brass; always promising to pay, promising to pay, tomorrow, and dying today, insolvent.*

—Henry David Thoreau, *Walden*

Introduction
Leibniz in Economics

All is for the best in this, the best of all possible worlds.
—Voltaire, *Candide, or Optimism*

he connection between labor and compensation, or between
those and any social or political entitlements, is not obvious, as
demonstrated by the historical reality of American slavery. Rather, an
argument always is needed in order to conclude that any specific set of
entitlements follows from a person's having produced a hard day's
work. Though it cost us a civil war and divergent social and political
legacies between North and South, the abolition of slavery was an
important precedent in what may be called the American morality of
labor. The end of slavery was one beginning toward recognition of the
equal humanity of dark-skinned people. But it was also a seed of
another fundamental principle of American freedom: that a human
being's labor is not worth nothing but, rather, is worth *some things*.

Societies must fuss incessantly over exactly what things honest
labor is worth. That is so because the valuation of labor is mainly a
cultural phenomenon. It is not about the revelation of any universal
truth of the matter, but it is about finding, or perhaps about bumbling
through trial and error upon, a social practice that accords with the
substantive limitations of economic life and, within that, a people's
moral sense of themselves. There are valuations of labor, usually part
of a larger political system or philosophy, whose practice makes stable
human society impossible or of an indefensibly poor quality.
Advanced capitalist democracies, such as the United States, do not

face this particular political problem. In such nations, there is no pretense that the valuation of labor is so open or undetermined that it could cast doubt over the necessity of the free market conditions that keep them safe and enriched. Rather, for such nations the main issue is balancing the market demands of labor with the social expectations of laboring people. To this end, capitalist societies simultaneously value labor in two very different ways—one is economic, the other, moral.

According to the economic valuation, labor has no inherent value. Labor is a mere commodity to be bought and sold, much in accordance with the same laws of supply and demand that regulate the distribution of all commercial goods. The laborer, consequently, enjoys no special consideration within the economic valuation of labor; such moral reservations threaten to disturb the incomparable efficiency that is promised in allowing free markets to absolutely determine the price of individual labor. The economic valuation of labor also treats certain moral facts about the world as inconsequential. For example, the fact that the average American will spend more than one-third of his existence working or that her particular work fulfills needs that are essential to the quality of American communal life are, within the economic valuation, of little relevance.

Again, that the going rate of one's full-time labor falls beneath what is needed in order to live decently by American standards, or that the amount of work one must perform to afford items of decency renders the proper raising of a family or caring for one's parents in old age impossible are, within the economic valuation, empirical data of no special significance. Within that perspective, all this information reveals is that some Americans will inevitably find themselves on the underside of the economy, having brought to the marketplace skills that are either currently in large supply or outmoded, driving down the value of what can be obtained for their exchange.

The economic valuation of labor does not concern itself at all with what might be called the "justness" of labor relations, except to ensure that labor transactions occur between individuals who freely enter into them. If the abolition of slavery in America was an important part of establishing the proposition that labor is not worth nothing, the economic valuation of labor agrees and states affirmatively that *labor is worth—and only worth—whatever can be bought with what others are willing pay for it, however much or little that is.*

The economic valuation of labor is central to the prosperity of the United States. Any economic history of the United States that is worth its salt will prove this many times over. But in embracing this irresistible truth, no nation should dismiss out of hand this question: what follows when goods and services that can be bought with full-time labor generally fall beneath a people's own ideals of fairness and social decency?

The claim to fame of the United States—the "Land of Opportunity"—is that nearly any person can make a decent life for themselves and their family through their labor. But a nation does not become one of "opportunity" simply because its citizens can obtain full-time jobs. Many nations are chock-full of individuals who work full-time or more, yet they also spend their entire lives toiling without even the possibility of stable living. Rather, "opportunity" is a two-way street: it is a relationship between individuals and institutions, between laborers and employers, and, ultimately, between citizens and governments.

If the United States is, in fact, a Land of Opportunity for workers, it is because the entire society is committed to ensuring that individuals who work hard enjoy rewards in accordance with Americans' senses of what is fair and right. Each time an American finds himself or herself unable to earn a decent life through their full-time work, however, the United States becomes a little more like those other places—the places Americans experience outrage over after reading the *New York Times* or watching *60 Minutes*, the places where it appears that citizens exist to serve government rather than the other way around.

Not all forms of low-compensation labor are morally disconcerting to Americans, however. Few teenagers who work full-time can expect to earn wages that will enable them to afford the things associated with the American dream—a home in a safe neighborhood, the resources needed to raise a family, a retirement plan. Indeed, a well-received argument against minimum-wage laws supposes that their primary effect is to dramatically decrease youth employment opportunities because employers are generally reluctant to pay higher wages for unskilled labor. Yet the United States has minimum-wage laws, and there appears to be no social concern whatsoever that working-age youth have suffered any loss of opportunity or other injustice with regard to employment.[1]

Many other oddball classes of toiler are met with the same public disregard—the weekend inventor/tinkerer, the would-be entrepreneur, the aspiring artist, workaday clowns and carneys. Such labors may have simply escaped Americans' moral radar, but there is a more promising explanation. All these types of labor may be cast as "nontraditional," or rather "self-made," in that they fall outside the labor paths that our basic institutions encourage for the purpose of fulfilling anticipated societal needs.

Parents commonly share stories recalling what they had hoped or imagined their children would grow up to be. The aspirations commonly include doctor, lawyer, or educator. Rarely do such aspirations include venture capitalist, circus acrobat, or poet laureate. This is no coincidence. Such ambitions are intimately connected with parents' experience-based perceptions of the most reliable and rewarding economic opportunities that American society has to offer. Invariably, the recommended path is to work for someone else—a public or private capitalist—in need of employees whose talents are historically highly compensated: doctors and lawyers. Educators, who receive far less compensation and social status, represent the pinnacle of job stability, and, as state employees, they often enjoy employee benefits packages that are better than those available in the private sphere.

Still, other classes of traditional labor are peripheral to the concerns of *The Unaffordable Nation* because of the transitory nature either of the work or the associated labor pool. A good example of this is the work study, where interns are employed and work for only very short-term gains. These employees typically lack interest in securing from their employment the pay and benefits necessary for long-term economic stability or in offering the substantial commitment to advancing the employer's best interest required to obtain such favorable employment terms.

In contrast to these groups, the main subjects of *The Unaffordable Nation* are emancipated adults dependent upon their occupations, their employers, and the government regulation of both to earn as needed for decent lives. That is most of us.

Questioning the "decency" of labor compensation opens the door to a set of considerations that, placed alongside the sheer force of the economic valuation of labor, often appears as irrational demands for higher wages and benefits. Too often, complaints about what life costs and felt senses of entitlement to greater resources in exchange for full-time work seem motivated by economic envy rather than an intelligible, realizable account of economic justice.[2] The cogency of what I shall call the "moral valuation of labor" suffers still more in the hands of those who confuse it for an alternative to, rather than a conditional modification of, the economic valuation of labor.

In truth, the moral valuation of labor is something of a luxury; its very possibility depends upon a level of economic prosperity that to date is only available to a select few free societies, of which the United States is one. The moral valuation of labor rests upon two assumptions, neither of which is grandiose or very broad-sweeping: first, labor has something like intrinsic value in American culture, which will often recommend rewarding some labor above its going rate in the marketplace; second, it will often be possible to reward some labor at this higher, moral rate without substantially interrupting the economic dynamism and incentives needed for the United States to remain among the most powerful free market nations in the world.

The moral valuation of labor is backed by an American cultural proviso that rivals the American people's commitment to largely unrestricted markets: in America, individuals who do great things should grow rich, individuals who do their parts should grow stable, and individuals who do not do their parts should starve. By this, the moral valuation of labor concludes that not only is labor not worth nothing, but *labor—at least full-time labor—is worth the elements of a decent American life, whatever that currently costs.*

The economic and moral valuations of labor commonly issue in conflicting social policy directives. The economic valuation of labor calls for government to protect the relatively natural system of matching labor supply and demand, mainly by not interjecting itself directly through labor regulations such as minimum-wage laws or indirectly through social welfare and tax benefit programs. The moral valuation of labor calls for government to ensure that, wherever possible, free markets value individual labor—and laborers—as do the American people. This can be accomplished directly through labor regulations such as minimum-wage laws or indirectly through social welfare and tax benefit programs meant to bring the costs of decent living into line with the average American's economic resources, including wages, but also by mandating meal and break periods, health and safety regulations, protecting rights to union activity, and so on.

In terms of global markets and international trade, the two valuations of labor reveal very different interests and attitudes toward practices that, however efficient economically, appear detrimental to the short-term or long-term well-being of the American labor force. Leading among these concerns are the trends of outsourcing certain services and production to nations where labor costs are extremely low relative to the United States, resulting in troubling phenomena such as the replacement of historically high-paying, skilled manufacturing jobs with low-wage, unskilled service positions.

The tension between economic and moral valuations of labor could be described as a "problem" or a "crisis," but such descriptions do not add value. Such nomenclature does not tell us anything about how to proceed in the face of disagreement. There is likewise no point in calling for the abandonment of one or the other ethic, or attempting to force them into the categories of "right" and "wrong." Having granted the real constraints and preconditions of economic prosperity—which underdetermine the relationship between labor and compensation—there remains only what Americans can and cannot live with.

For example, commerce in the United States survived the virtual elimination of child labor imposed by the passage of the Fair Labor Standards Act in 1938. This, even though child labor was then and remains a robust source of cheap unskilled labor that, within the right cultural constraints, is remarkably stable. The United States has not considered relaxing prohibitions on child labor as a solution to the nation's reliance upon immigrant laborers, who fill positions that even poor American adults will not accept; this speaks volumes about the morality of labor that America is practicing. Instead, like many other nations, America supports massive public expenditures on social welfare programs and progressive taxation intended, in part, to shore up those who are the hardworking unsuccessful: well-meaning, industrious persons who have suffered poor luck, poor justice, and to some extent, poor choice.

Cultural moralities are pendular, rocking between moral extremes conditioned by social and historical circumstances, but hopefully they come to rest at not-too-unhappy mediums. What I describe as the American morality of labor is no exception. *The Unaffordable Nation* is necessary now because the United States is swinging too far toward the view that the economic valuation of labor is all there is. While the economic valuation of labor is rightly ascendant, the view becomes extreme when it is supposed that in the United States it is no longer possible—or wise, fair, or warranted—to adjust economic arrangements for the express moral purpose of improving the relationship between labor and compensation. The quality of the lives of America's citizen laborers seems no longer to be a genuine public concern.

The demands of successful capitalist democracy already make for relatively thin senses of community. The assertion that the United States can no longer afford to support an acceptable, normative connection between labor and compensation is altogether different in kind, however. That move represents the total eclipse of anything that might be recognizable as a community. In effect, it is to declare as passé the notion that the good citizen, who does what is asked of him or her in terms of work, deserves anything, much less a decent life, in return.

As the conditions for many working Americans worsen despite their industriousness, there is an unmistakable air of celebration, victory, and comeuppance among some Americans, who interpret these developments as setting things right not just for themselves, but for all. It is a curious sort of argument, one that emboldens some to look struggling Americans in the eyes and to say to them with confidence that the stagnation of their wages and general loss of economic well-being despite their hard work is actually part of the economic improvement of the United States. This book calls into question the notions that *this* economic America is the just and right one, and that nothing more could or should be done for general American workers.

It is likely that few Americans have ever heard of Gottfried Leibniz. In brief, Leibniz (1646–1716) was a German polymath whose legacy includes the invention of calculus apart from Isaac Newton and his laudable contributions in fields as diverse as physics, psychology, engineering and logic, and in multiple languages no less. Leibniz was primarily a lawyer and a philosopher, however, he was most famous for his defense of a doctrine known as religious "optimism."[3] In an attempt to reconcile an all-powerful Christian God with the existence of evil and other worldly imperfections, Leibniz argued that men must "live in the best of all possible worlds," because this world is the creation of an absolutely perfect God. If Leibniz is right, there is no point in trying to remedy the human condition because there is no improving upon perfection. If, as Leibniz reasoned, the suffering of the world is an integral though incomprehensible part of God's perfect plan, we should do nothing other than acquiesce in these mysteries of faith. Famine, disease, violence, corruption—all perfect.

I introduce Leibniz because something like his doctrine of optimism is, today, the leading moral justification for the economic status quo in the United States. The mantra of what I call "economic optimism" in the United States is that this America is the "best of all economic worlds." According to the mantra, it is impossible for major American corporations to forego any profit to improve the buying power of their employees or to demonstrate a sincere commitment to the well-being of the hands that help in their success. Likewise, it is futile for government to attempt any progressive plan of action to soften the individual consequences of inadequate wages and the rising costs of everything basic to the American dream.[4]

Rather, the existing economic conditions are absolutely "perfect"— understood as (or near) the best that anyone could hope for or reasonably expect—and things could only be improved through still freer markets and substantially less government. Among the perfections:

- *Stagnated Wages*: A recent Employment Cost Index, which measures the labor costs of all US civilian workers, found that total compensation—wages plus benefits—grew 3.1 percent between the fourth quarters of 2004 and 2005, the slowest rate of growth since 1999. Over the same period, however, inflation grew 3.4 percent, which means real compensation actually fell by 0.3 percent. Likewise, in 2005 nominal wages (the wages paid rather than the actual buying power of those wages) raised an average of 2.4 percent, which, alongside 3.4 percent inflation, means that real wages fell nearly a full percent in 2005. By comparison, in 2005 the average CEO earned 821 times as much as the minimum-wage earner, earning more before lunchtime on the first day of work than the minimum-wage earner took home for the entire year.[5]
- *Poverty for Some Full-Time Work*: The federal minimum wage has not increased since September 1997, resting at the lowly rate of $5.15 per hour.[6] Most states have their own minimum-wage laws that are more aggressive, however. For example, the 2007 minimum wage in the state of Oregon is $7.80 per hour. These

rates make only $10,712 and $16,224 annually. I believe all would agree that prevailing minimum wages are inadequate to live decently, however one prefers to define "decent."

- *Unaffordability of Health Insurance*: Premiums for employer-based health insurance rose by 9.2 percent in 2005 (the fifth consecutive year of increases above 9 percent) and 7.7 percent in 2006. All types of health plans, whether Health Maintenance Organization (HMO), Preferred Provider Organization (PPO), or (Point Of Service plan) POS, reflected the increase. Premiums continue to increase much faster than overall inflation (3.5 percent) and wage gains (3.8 percent). The annual premium that a health insurer charges an employer for a health plan covering a family of four averaged $10,800 in 2005 and $11,480 in 2006. Workers on average contributed $2,713 in 2005 and $2,973 in 2006 for their health plans. The annual premiums for family coverage exceed the gross earnings of a full-time, federal minimum-wage worker ($10,712). Overall, employment-based health insurance premiums have increased 87 percent since 2000. By comparison, cumulative inflation and wages grew only 14 percent and 15 percent, respectively. Notably, 2006 was the third consecutive year that premium increases were less than the previous year, yet health insurance premiums continue to increase twice as fast as wages.[7]
- *Decline of the Middle Class*: A recent Brookings Institution study shows that between 1970 and 2000, middle-income neighborhoods as a proportion of all metropolitan neighborhoods declined from 58 percent to 41 percent; the percentage of lower-income families who lived in middle-income neighborhoods shrank from 55 percent to 37 percent, indicating substantial segregation of lower-income and higher-income neighborhoods; in general, middle-class neighborhoods and metropolitan areas are shrinking much faster than the proportion of middle-income families in America, and fewer and fewer centrally located neighborhoods in metropolitan areas admit of middle-income families at all.[8]

"All for the best in this," proclaims the Optimist, and whatever is objectionable about such data must be blamed on government regulation (or so the mantra says). It would follow that there is no point to increasing minimum wages, readjusting upward corporate tax burdens, re-liberalizing bankruptcy laws for individuals in addition to corporations, socializing healthcare, or attempting to mitigate for American workers the inevitable hardships of necessary globalization; these could only make things worse for those failing by their hard work. According to economic optimists, the working disadvantaged need to accept their inability to afford decent lives through full-time work because, although it may be incomprehensible to them, such states of affair are part of a divine American economic order that cannot be improved upon.

In his book *Development as Freedom*, the Nobel laureate economist Amartya Sen has commented on the ascent of economic optimism:

> "It is the customary fate of new truths," says T. H. Huxley in *Science and Culture*, "to begin as heresies and to end as superstitions." There was a time—not very long ago—when every young economist "knew" in what respects the market systems has serious limitations: all the textbooks repeated the same list of "defects." The intellectual rejection of the market mechanism often led to radical proposals for altogether different methods of organizing the world (sometimes involving a powerful bureaucracy and unimagined physical burdens), without serious examination of the possibility that the proposed alternatives might involve even bigger failures than the markets were expected to produce. There was, often enough, rather little interest in the new and additional problems that the alternative arrangements may create. The intellectual climate has changed quite dramatically over the last few decades, and the tables are now turned. The virtues of the market mechanism are now standardly assumed to be so pervasive that qualifications seem unimportant. Any pointer to the defects of the market mechanism appears to be, in the present mood, strangely old-fashioned and contrary to con-

temporary culture (like playing an old 78 rpm record with music from the 1920s). One set of prejudices has given way to another—opposite—set of preconceptions. Yesterday's unexamined faith has become today's heresy, and yesterday's heresy is now the new superstition.[9]

The pursuit of economic justice is impossible in a culture espousing this kind of optimism. That pursuit presupposes the existence of options and room for improvement, things that are absent in a nation that is already finished. If economic optimism were true, then pleas for economic relief by hardworking Americans would be unintelligible *metaphysically*, akin to political demands for weightlessness in a world where the laws of gravity obtain.

Economic optimism faces an obvious challenge, however. To any apparent contradiction between the Christian God and the human condition, the Christian optimist can always respond that "God assuredly always chooses the best." On what divine power do economic optimists rely in order to explain apparent contradictions between this America and the American dream? That is, who—or what—is the God of economic optimism? It is the science of economics, of course. The doctrine of economic optimism assumes that economic knowledge is heading for purposes of structuring human affairs. Contrary ways of thinking and categories of knowledge must stand down.

For example, consider the surreptitious role of economic optimism in the intellectual tradition known as law and economics, whose normative goal is to fix public policy according to one or another conception of economic efficiency. Undeniably, law and economics scholarship continues to yield a wealth of valuable information regarding the economic consequences of legal rules, many of which can be anticipated and so factored into public policy decision making.

But however valuable law and economic scholarship has proven in its own right, the movement itself enjoys an artificial predominance built upon economic optimism, with the result that this scholarly tradition is often seen to be the final word on public policy questions rather than what it truly is, namely, the careful articulation of one set of considerations to be balanced against every other. The unspoken reliance upon economic optimism diverts attention away from the *priority* of such concerns in public policy decisions.

The economic optimist, presented with apparent contradictions between, on the one hand, the commonplace insufficiency of labor to earn decent wages and, on the other hand, workers fulfilling American dreams, confidently replies, "Free markets assuredly always choose the best." Indeed, free markets very often do choose best, certainly better than government does. But it is possible for the wisest choices of free markets to press too heavily upon the aims of distributive justice, requiring societies to decide whether marginal gains in labor productivity and gross products promised by particular policies is worth often unacknowledged sacrifices in individual well-being. National increases in labor productivity and gross products, for example, can be the result of compelling individuals to work longer hours with new technology for less pay and benefits. Such measures become unequivocally positive indicators of the health of economy only after granting certain other assumptions that may not always hold, especially at the level of individual work.

To return to the point, there is no room for the moral valuation of labor in a world of economic optimism. There is no room for the proviso that Americans who do their part should grow stable from it nor the conviction that Americans who work full-time and are modest in their economic waste are entitled to decent lives in return.

Leibniz introduced his doctrine of religious optimism in 1710. In 1759 an Enlightenment philosopher named François-Marie Arouet, better known as Voltaire (1694–1778), penned the satire *Candide, or Optimism*.[10] Voltaire means to expose the absurdity of religious optimism by confronting the horrors of eighteenth-century life, including the Lisbon earthquake of 1755, which resulted in ninety thousand deaths (more than one-third of the population of Lisbon at the time). Needless to say, in the end the trials of the character Candide leave him a living refutation of religious optimism. Such trials are too numerous and involved to recount here, but readers only need to imagine what must have occurred in order for one of Candide's companions to proclaim, "I would be glad to know which is worst, to be ravished a hundred times by Negro pirates, to have one buttock cut off, to run the gauntlet among the Bulgarians, to be whipped and hanged at an auto-da-fé, to be dissected, to be chained to an oar in a galley; and, in short, to experience all the miseries through which every one of us hath passed, or to remain here doing nothing?"[11]

There are many Americans whose lives, like Candide's, are living refutations of America's economic optimism. There are also many books available that document such lives.[12] In their own ways, these books call into question the doctrine of economic optimism or various social theories underlying it, which rationalize the worsening condition of hardworking Americans with the belief that this America is the best of all possible economic worlds for them.[13]

The Unaffordable Nation attempts add to this latter class of critique but in an entirely new way: by revisiting the American morality of labor—a morality that, among other things, finds the inability to afford items of decency through reasonable amounts of labor an unequivocal injustice.[14]

NOTES

1. For a challenging analysis of differences in youth employment opportunities resulting from changes in minimum wages, see John Abowd, Francis Kamarz, Thomas Lemieux, and David Margolis, "Minimum Wages and Youth Employment in France and the United States," in *Youth Employment and Joblessness in Advanced Countries*, ed. David Blanchflower and Richard Freeman, 427–72 (Chicago: University of Chicago Press, 2000).

2. "Human envy," Friedrich von Hayek writes, "is certainly not one of the sources of discontent that a free society can eliminate. It is probably one of the essential conditions for the preservation of such a society that we do not countenance envy, not sanction its demands by camouflaging it as social

justice, but treat it, in the words of John Stuart Mill, as 'the most anti-social and evil of all passions.'" Friedrich von Hayek, *The Constitution of Liberty* (Chicago: University of Chicago Press, 1960).

3. Gottfried Wilhelm Leibniz, *Theodicy: Essays on the Goodness of God, the Freedom of Man, and the Origins of Evil* (Chicago: Open Court, 1988).

4. For a poignant review of the broadly shared tenets of the American dream, see Jennifer Hochschild, *Race, Class, and the Soul of the Nation: Facing Up to the American Dream* (Princeton, NJ: Princeton University Press, 1995), pp. 15–38.

5. Jared Bernstein, "Wages Picture: Real Compensation Down as Wage Squeeze Continues," Economic Policy Institute, Jan. 31, 2006, http://www .epi.org/content.cfm/webfeat_econindicators_wages_20060131 (accessed September 20, 2006).

6. On February 1, 2007, Congress voted to increase the federal minimum wage to $7.25 per hour over the course of two years. The bill also includes tax breaks for small businesses. As of the date of this publication, the bill has not been finalized and delivered to President Bush for signature.

7. The Henry J. Kaiser Family Foundation and the Health Research Educational Trust, *Employee Health Benefits:2005 and 2006 Annual Surveys*.

8. Jason Booza, Jackie Cutsinger, and George Galster, "Where Did They Go?: The Decline of Middle-income Neighborhoods in Metropolitan America," Brookings Institution, June 2006, http://www.brook.edu/metro /pubs/20060622_middleclass.htm (accessed September 20, 2006). See also Janny Scott, "Cities Shed Middle Class, and Are Richer and Poorer for It," *New York Times*, July 23, 2006.

9. Amartya Sen, *Development as Freedom* (New York: Anchor Books, 1999), p. 111.

10. Voltaire, *Candide* (New York: Barnes & Noble Classics, 2003).

11. Ibid., p. 127.

12. See, e.g., Barbara Ehrenreich, *Nickel and Dimed: On (Not) Getting By in America* (New York: Metropolitan Books, 2001); Eileen Applebaum, Annette Bernhardt, and Richard Murnane, eds., *Low-Wage America: How Employers Are Reshaping Opportunity in the Workplace* (New York: Russell Sage Foundation, 2003); David Shipler, *The Working Poor: Invisible in America* (New York: Vintage Books, 2004); Chuck Collins and Felice

Yeskel, *Economic Apartheid in America: A Primer on Economic Inequality and Insecurity* (New York: New Press, 2005).

13. See, e.g., John Kenneth Galbraith's classic work, *The Affluent Society* (Boston: Houghton Mifflin, 1969).

14. *The Unaffordable Nation* shares very much, though not all, in philosophical spirit with Stuart White's *The Civic Minimum: On the Rights and Obligations of Economic Citizenship* (Oxford: Oxford University Press, 2003). Whereas White is writing for an exclusively academic audience, however, *The Unaffordable Nation* is a middling sort of book, exploring the same issues but at levels and using approaches designed to make them more accessible and engaging to a concerned citizenry. For that reason, I deliberately attempt to use readily accessible data sources that indicate support for the moral positions taken in the book without saturating readers in the full complexities (and literatures) of the underlying theoretical debates, which should come later. For interested parties, I also recommend Stephen Nathanson's *Economic Justice* (Upper Saddle River, NJ: Prentice-Hall, 1998).

PART 1:
THE UNAFFORDABLE NATION

By necessaries I understand not only the commodities which are indispensably necessary for the support of life, but whatever the custom of the country renders it indecent for creditable people, even of the lowest order, to be without. A linen shirt, for example, is, strictly speaking, not a necessary of life. The Greeks and Romans lived, I suppose, very comfortably though they had no linen. But in the present times, through the greater part of Europe, a creditable day-labourer would be ashamed to appear in public without a linen shirt, the want of which would be supposed to denote that disgraceful degree of poverty which, it is presumed, nobody can well fall into without extreme bad conduct. Custom, in the same manner, has rendered leather shoes a necessary of life in England. The poorest creditable person of either sex would be ashamed to appear in public without them. In Scotland, custom has rendered them a necessary of life to the lowest order of men; but not to the same order of women, who may, without any discredit, walk about barefooted. In France they are necessaries neither to men nor to women, the lowest rank of both sexes appearing there publicly, without any discredit, sometimes in wooden shoes, and sometimes barefooted. Under necessaries, therefore, I comprehend not only those things which nature, but those things which the established rules of decency have rendered necessary to the lowest rank of people. All other things I call luxuries, without meaning by this appellation to throw the smallest degree of reproach upon the temperate use of them. Beer and ale, for example, in Great Britain, and wine, even in the wine countries, I call luxuries. A man of any rank may, without any reproach, abstain totally from tasting such liquors. Nature does not render them necessary for the support of life, and custom nowhere renders it indecent to live without them.... Any

rise in the average price of necessaries, unless it is compensated by a proportionable rise in the wages of labour, must necessarily diminish more or less the ability of the poor to bring up numerous families, and consequently to supply the demand for useful labour, whatever may be the state of that demand, whether increasing, stationary, or declining, or such as requires an increasing, stationary, or declining population.
—Adam Smith, *The Wealth of Nations*

Introduction:
Products, Persons, and
Unaffordability

To claim that some product is "unaffordable" for some person is, unfortunately, a remarkably complex proposition. This is so because the concept captures multiple relationships between products and persons. If all that were meant by "unaffordability" when applied to any particular product x and person y was the brute observation that the resources at y's disposal are presently not adequate to purchase or otherwise legally obtain x, not much of interest would follow. Strictly speaking, there are many things most persons cannot afford. Few of us will ever be millionaires or own a mansion and a yacht. But the significance of unaffordability as a relationship between products and persons changes. It depends on the type of product that is unaffordable to the person and the type of person who cannot afford the product.

As for products, there is obviously great moral difference between the inability to afford a mansion and a yacht, the inability to afford a house and an automobile, and the inability to afford a rental in a safe neighborhood that is also near public transportation. The inability to afford the first pair of goods perhaps deprives one of the upper crust. The inability to afford the second pair of goods deprives one of a part of the American dream but also of economic opportunities available only to those who can reliably travel. The inability to afford the third pair of goods is an indication that one is altogether deprived of a mainstream American existence and the cultural quality of life associated with it, if not the ability to ensure survival at all. Put differently, when

35

speaking of the inability to afford particular products, it matters
whether the products are considered items of *luxury*, *decency*, or
necessity.

Following Adam Smith, this book is not mainly concerned with
items of luxury or items of necessity merely but rather is concerned
with items of "decency." Smith defines these as items of necessity
without which human beings would perish or be unable to manage
stable society, *plus* everything else that the society in question determines, as matters of custom, to be goods indispensable to its particular
mode of civilization. As was true of Smith's England, in America
today a good linen shirt and a presentable pair of leather shoes are
items of decency that are absolutely necessary if one is to effectively
participate in American culture and economy. Beer, wine, and ale—
not so much.

Under this approach, a life is not made decent because it is spiritu-
ally fulfilled or in accord with a person's preferences. Nor is a life decent
because it successfully carries out any particular design for which it
arguably exists, religious or otherwise teleological. To claim that a life
is decent is merely to observe that, other things being equal, the life
itself should not fail for lack of access to those resources that social
custom identifies as necessary in order to function effectively within the
society in question. Therefore, a decent life is one that admits of adequate stores of decent items or commensurate resources, as customarily
defined by a people. Here, as defined by the American people.

The items that Americans identify as customarily decent are
important because together they establish, in democratic fashion, the
standard for determining what counts as a decent quality of life. It is
with reference to this standard of decency that Americans assign
weights and priorities to all manner of public concerns and policies
over economy, including the regulation and distribution of products.

As for persons, the reasons why items of decency are unaffordable
also matter. In the passage above, Smith reveals that the ability of citizens to afford items of decency is intimately connected with individual wages and the prices of items. Where the prices of items of

decency increase but wages and related resources do not, Smith predicts corresponding declines in the quality of the nation's labor pool. But Smith hints at another, distinct harm to workers caused by unaffordability that is central to our subject—*indignity*. Smith observes that in his England, the lack of access to certain products made one *less creditable* to his or her countrymen and served as independent sources of shame and disgrace, because possession and dispossession of such products was received by the English as indicative of moral character. In his own words, there are certain products "the want of which would be supposed to denote that disgraceful degree of poverty which, it is presumed, nobody can well fall into without extreme bad conduct."

In Smith's England, a person unable to afford items of decency was, by moral definition, a bad person. As will be seen later, the United States has inherited from England this cultural predilection. That is, in the Land of Opportunity, it is generally presumed that only defective persons are unable afford items of decency. This conclusion depends upon a certain, exceptionally strong presumption of freedom regarding Americans' ability to control their environment. The presumption casts Americans as radically free and undetermined, making success or failure purely a function of individual choice. The strong presumption of freedom that Americans endorse interprets impoverished and indecent lives to be wholly optional; one is always capable of avoiding this path through individual action. It would follow that persons who cannot afford items of decency deserve the indignity they publicly suffer, which is but the proper response to a human being's choice to refrain from earning items of decency for himself or herself.

Presumptions about freedom are existential in nature. They comprise a part of how people order their moral universe. Fortunately, Americans have access to the experiences needed to consciously temper their presumptions about freedom. From experience, Americans know that *poor choice* is not the only reason items of decency might become unaffordable for a person. Americans know that the same can occur due to *poor justice* or *poor luck*. The cause of one's inability to afford a mansion and a yacht may be having squandered one's inheritance or refusing, though able, to work well—poor choice; or having been legally excluded from education or job opportunities that, given one's natural talents, might have yielded such an earning prospectus—poor justice; or having been born with labor-limiting physical or cognitive disabilities, or into an economic milieu unfavorable to one's most marketable ideas—poor luck.

The inability to afford a house and an automobile, or a safe rental on public transit lines, is also traceable most immediately to poor choice, poor justice, or poor luck, or some combination thereof, but it is not always exclusively nor predominantly a factor of poor choice. Because of their strong presumption of freedom, however, Americans are not very careful about distinguishing poor choice, poor justice, and poor luck cases. As a consequence, the indignity of unaffordability is heaved upon nearly any person who is unable to afford items of decency, regardless of the true causes.

In simplified form, all of the above represent a moral calculus of sorts, which finds that items of decency are crucial to public respect and dignity in America. Individuals who cannot afford items of decency suffer the associated indignity of unaffordability. But for some of these people—increasingly many, it seems—the cause of unaffordability is not their own poor choice. It is the fact that the nation itself has grown unaffordable.

Chapters 1 and 2 contend, by example, that the inability to afford items of decency—whether due to poor choice, poor justice, or poor luck—has unappreciated social costs. As already explained, Americans have two distinct reasons to want items of decency: such items constitute of the quality of life that Americans customarily expect for themselves and their brethren. The possession of such products comprises a badge of public dignity, the lack of which disassociates the deprived from the rest of America's moral community. Given the gravity of these reasons for wanting items of decency, how do Americans react when they find themselves unable to obtain such goods? Do they simply accept their lot? Will expressions of dissatisfaction with their circumstances be restricted to constructive economic conduct and established forms of political protest? Or do such persons turn to more desperate and destructive measures? There is evidence that the social costs of unaffordability are substantial. The current roles that lawsuits and lotteries play in American culture and Americans' increasing reliance upon credit in lieu of suitable labor rewards are only two examples.

Chapter 3 returns to the notion of "decent lives," examining some poignant criticisms of the ideal offered nearly one hundred years ago by the social Darwinist William Graham Sumner. Considering and answering Sumner's objections to the ideal of decent lives adds clarity to the shared American expectations regarding the quality of life that should generally be available to persons who work hard. Finally, chapter 4 investigates the mechanisms and forces at work beneath the unaffordable nation, locating such causes ultimately in politics rather than in any objective constraints of the marketplace. At least at this stage, the identification of politics as the cause of the unaffordable nation carries no pejorative connotation. This only captures how certain disagreements regarding how best to balance capitalism with democracy can have calamitous consequences upon other national priorities, in this case, affordability with labor.

CHAPTER 1
Of Lawsuits and Lotteries

In the matter of making a living, many Americans intuit little difference between lawsuits and lotteries, and they carry a perverse understanding of each. The lawsuit is not just a method of resolving inevitable disputes over serious rights.[1] Nor are lotteries just a mode of recreation to be indulged only sporadically, after one's bills are paid.[2] Each undertaking also represents an opportunity—a remote chance for a degree of financial security that, to many Americans, seems beyond their reach through mere hard work and financial discipline.

I shall argue that the abuse of lawsuits and lotteries is a foreseeable consequence of unaffordability with labor. Lawsuits and lotteries are activities that individuals *may choose* as a means of obtaining income. Each is a strategic, economic choice that, while risky and even when abused, remains in some ways more respectable and less conspicuous than accepting private charity or soliciting public welfare. Overplaying the lottery or gambling and undertaking frivolous litigation, then, are strangely consistent with American beliefs about freedom and the power of individuals to control their environment. While they are deliberate choices, lawsuit and lottery abuse are also responses. Such choices are opportunistic overreactions to the experience of unaffordability with labor. The lawsuit abuser typically has suffered a genuine offense, albeit one that common sense and decency recommends to let slide or to settle outside the legal system. And lottery abusers, like many gambling addicts, often pass into habitude only amid financial hardships that make the activity more seductive than amid financial security. We will discuss each in turn.

41

❧

> The position we have now reached is this: starting from the State, we try to remedy the failures of all the families, all the nurseries, all the schools, all the workshops, all the secondary institutions that once had some authority of their own. Everything is ultimately brought into the Law Courts. We are trying to stop the leak at the other end.
> —G. K. Chesterton, *Illustrated London News*, March 24, 1923

A common criticism of the United States is that it is an "overlitigious" society. This allegation is ambiguous, however, because the term has two meanings, only one of which has held the attention of the public. The first definition, which is the focus of state and federal reforms, refers to the phenomenon of more claims being filed and more relief being granted than is optimal if the civil justice system is to keep pace with some predetermined set of institutional goals. According to this definition, overlitigiousness can exist even if all plaintiffs' attorneys only took cases on good-faith bases and all Americans behaved conservatively regarding the types of offenses that justify legal action.

This definition has radical-sounding implications, for it can recommend the rejection of potentially valid moral and legal claims and the circumscription of potentially justifiable degrees of relief for the sake of other, more important goals. It is hard to imagine goals so valuable that they are worth trading some portion of the very ends for which the justice system exists. The definition loses whatever sex appeal it may have had when it is admitted that the value that takes pride of place over the open moral evaluation of legal claims is ... insurance costs. If the argument is to be accepted, however, it is possible for goodhearted citizens to receive more legal relief than they really want and for juries to award more damages than what is best for society once the full social costs of such substantial justice are made clear.

It turns out that no justice against corporations is free, but rather it is only gained at an individual premium that is proportionate to the liability corporations pay for their wrongdoing. The bad corporation, justly found guilty and civilly penalized, will have to pay more in order to insure against future claims like the one just suffered and therefore will move the increased costs in the only direction it knows how—downward, to consumers.

Now multiply this effect for every corporation with good products and poor conduct. It is only a matter of time before the costs of insurance needed to enter into these particular markets will grow prohibitive; well-meaning, non-offending, but smaller companies will be squeezed out. Those that can afford to remain in the market will spend less on innovation and employ fewer people, and the lack of market diversity will winnow the range of products and undercut healthy price competition. And this is all supposedly because some Americans want to be justly compensated for losing an arm on the job through faulty machinery, for consuming a product later discovered to cause stroke, or for receiving less than what is due in pay or promotions because of race.

Set aside for a moment the idea that Americans should want less in damages for these kinds of harms because getting too much relief can result in companies producing less of the things that Americans want access to. For Americans who do not smoke but have claims against cigarette companies for the effects of second-hand smoke, perhaps this is not the best argument. But what about claims against hospitals or medical staff with the knowledge that too many big claims may result in some Americans not having access to the levels of care or number of good doctors needed to service their neighborhoods?

There is still another problem to consider. Many people will behave irrationally about these matters. They will not see that in a world where insurance functions as it does, everyone might be better off demanding a little less monetary justice. Others will be free riders, seeking harmful amounts of monetary justice in hopes that everyone else will absorb the cost of damages awarded.

Faced with these obstacles, an intelligent plan might be to pass legislation designed to limit access to justice—claims as well as relief—paring it down to the levels needed to ensure that the insurance costs of doing business remain low enough that individuals and companies will still find it worthwhile to enter into promising markets. Some argue that the positive effects of reigning in this kind of overlitigiousness are everywhere, with Texas as a leading example of medical malpractice reform. According to the American Tort Reform Association, Texas enacted sweeping tort reforms in 2003, establishing limits on noneconomic and punitive damages in products liability, medical malpractice, and class action cases. In 2005, just a couple of years later, the five largest Texas insurers cut rates, some by as much as 17 percent, and malpractice insurance premiums have dropped correspondingly, saving upwards of $50 million in insurance premiums. Also, some counties have seen dramatic rises in the number of doctors, including doctors in high-risk specialty areas. Perhaps most telling, malpractice claims themselves have been halved.[3]

This is how the story goes if "overlitigiousness" is defined only as an inefficient degree of administrative claims and fees. It is a story that is quite persuasive, as far as stories go, but it is woefully inadequate in the end. For, supposing things work exactly as described above, there remains the problem of individual choice. Individual choice arises not simply regarding the conceptions of justice that lead plaintiffs and juries to conclude that certain harms are worth damages that would afford a plaintiff the life of a Rockefeller or a Vanderbilt. It also arises in regard to the frequency of "frivolous" lawsuits.

The supposition that some lawsuits are frivolous imputes to those filing the complaints (and perhaps to their attorneys) an awareness of the invalidity of certain claims, or—more interesting—a perverted sense of justice that leads persons either to manufacture or grossly exaggerate the degrees of harms they have suffered. On such complex subjects of moral character, tort reform laws are near silent. Tort reform laws become a partial and only prophylactic response to "over-litigiousness" when that term is defined not merely as an excessive number of claims and amounts demanded for relief but as a moral character defect. This motivates some plaintiffs' attorneys and litigants to engage the civil justice system for illegitimate purposes, attempting to exploit it for profit rather than serving justice.

It is possible that within the confines of effective tort reform there remains a nation of opportunists still on the lookout for get-rich scams. Morally speaking, if the United States were a nation of criminals, we would not be contented by the mere fact that the criminal laws worked so well that we barely noticed. Rather, even if the law prevented most crimes, we would be deeply troubled by the knowledge that so many Americans were searching for opportunities to commit them. So the same with tort reform laws. Preventing individuals from accessing certain types of claims and certain amounts of relief leaves virtually untouched the character issues motivating such poor conduct to begin with.

One rationale for tort reform laws gets at this deeper moral issue via the suggestion that the prospect of extremely large damage awards is causally linked to, if not the primary incentive driving, frivolous litigation. A related but different assumption is that the moral defect of overlitigiousness would not exist, or would be far less pervasive, if the prospect of large damage awards was absent. However, these observations cannot resurrect tort reform as any kind of solution to lawsuit abuse interpreted as a defect of national character. While the prospect of growing rich likely creates a substantial incentive to pursue questionable litigation, the prospect of growing rich is probably unnecessary to create a sufficient incentive to engage in the same or similar conduct. I mean to suggest that the prospect of being *temporarily less poor* or of *feeling less economically insecure*, even if there is absolutely no prospect of growing rich, could for many persons provide sufficient enticement to undertake frivolous litigation.

If this is true, then the amounts of damages needed to entice unscrupulous plaintiffs and attorneys to go forward will prove far less than the huge amounts of damages that juries occasionally award. They pursue these claims not be become rich but to become financially stable.

Likewise, recognizing overlitigiousness as one species of disrespect for the procedural rule of law shifts the goals of reform. From an external view of the law and its ends, perhaps erecting adequate barriers and imposing other disincentives to filing claims is all that is necessary in the short term. From an internal view of the law, as an institution whose success depends upon respect for the rule of law, the larger question is how and why Americans have come to believe either that the threshold of offense that justifies legal action is so low or that something about their social circumstances or public life generally makes the frivolous pursuit of litigation a marginal rather than a serious moral offense. This is a sociological question, and the lack of an answer prevents law from establishing an enlightened, inter-institutional approach to overlitigiousness as a cultural problem, much like obesity in America.

In the absence of a definitive answer, I am suggesting that a primary incentive for lawsuit (and lottery) abuse in the United States is the indignity of unaffordability. The desire to belong to the class of the economically respectable—or to appear that way—and to enjoy the lifestyle of the financially stable, is worth risking ever-greater financial hardship. From the vantage point of such desperate persons, the risk is actually a small one. Often, they will have already concluded that they lack the power to reverse their economic circumstances. Unsuccessful lawsuits and lotteries are but additional evidence of their believed economic impotence. Successful lawsuits and lotteries, on the other hand, symbolize a fresh start. They are a break in the otherwise uninterrupted reality of disadvantage, revealing prospects of normalcy.

In their groundbreaking work examining increases in discrimination lawsuits throughout the 1970s and 1980s, John Donahue and Peter Siegelman found that a key factor in discrimination lawsuit-filing rates was the unemployment rate. That is, throughout the 1970s and 1980s, filing rates of discrimination claims rose and fell with the rates of unemployment.[4] Unaffordability with labor is different than unaffordability resulting from unemployment, of course. Moreover, Donahue and Siegelman identified many other factors that influenced the filing rates of discrimination lawsuits during this period, such as declines in unions and the fact that minorities were less likely to lodge complaints from fear of losing recently gained employment opportunities.

Still, there remains an obvious connection between unemployment and unaffordability with labor as incentives to litigation, namely, loss of the opportunity to procure through one's labor the resources needed to obtain items of decency and the social standing that comes with them. Far from unreasonable, it makes common sense to think that the inability of meeting one's decent needs through labor will result in similar, if only weaker, incentives.

Donahue and Siegelman's most recent work suggests that the incentives to litigation created by unaffordability with labor may prove quite powerful in present-day America. In exploring whether the connection between unemployment and discrimination lawsuit-filing rates held for the 1990s, they found just the opposite: in the 1990s the filing rates for discrimination claims rose in spite of relatively low unemployment rates. To account for this shift, the authors concluded that there are incentives for litigation today that were not a force in the 1970s and 1980s, such as the Civil Rights Act of 1991 and shifts in the composition of discrimination suits.

Of import here, the authors also concluded that the harms of discrimination are increasingly measured in terms of lost utility and dignity rather than in lost income or earnings.[5] Modern workers are much more sensitive to "dignitary" as opposed to strictly "economic" harms than even a few decades ago. They have come to view certain workplace treatment—treatment that demonstrates respect for them as laborers—as tantamount to rights. Furthermore, they are prepared to sue to vindicate such harms even where the amounts of economic damage attributable to employers is marginal.

This, and Donahue and Siegelman's observation that the volume of discrimination cases filed in federal courts nearly doubled between 1992 and 1997, fits neatly with the notion that indignity of unaffordability is an incentive for litigation. The inability of Americans to afford items of decency through labor is a constant attack upon their senses of self-worth. The indignity of unaffordability will not express itself in pure form, however. There is as yet no actionable "tort of unaffordability" under which hardworking but failing Americans can seek relief in law courts against their employers or the government. And that would be a bad idea for the reasons noted by G. K. Chesterton at the beginning of this chapter.

Still, given this unique feature of the American economic identity, one should expect this special kind of indignity to fuel and exaggerate the harm of every other workplace offense that is legally actionable upon a certain showing of facts such as discrimination, wrongful discharge, and the like. In the failing laborer's mind, the floating indignity of unaffordability is always available to compound any other workplace harm, thus lowering the moral threshold that must be met to make legal action justifiable for any alleged violation. From this perspective, even minor or isolated employer misconduct may be interpreted by the laborer as the final straw in a system of inequality that began with having to accept labor under terms of which both parties knew the laborer could not afford to live decently. The laborer is not even recognized for the decision to avoid crime or other untoward means of getting a living, including lawsuits (or lottery) abuse.

If the above is correct, tort reform laws do indeed perform a valuable service. They bring within tolerable levels the extent to which lawsuit abusers are successful in their acts of dignitary revolt, preventing them from burying desirable markets under unmanageable insurance costs. This is akin to preventing the child on a street full of candy stores from consuming too many sweets by locking the doors on most of the shops. On the other hand, tort reform laws do nothing whatsoever to alleviate the underlying motivations of lawsuit abuse. Just as the candy-craving child will keep an eye out for candy stores left unlocked and steal away into any shop that has inadvertently left its door ajar, the lawsuit abuser likewise remains on the prowl for the big score and will circumvent law at other opportunities for the same end.

This is law from the viewpoint of "the bad man." In "The Path of the Law," Oliver Wendell Holmes Jr. famously writes, "If you want to know the law and nothing else, you must look at it as a bad man, who cares only for the material consequences which such knowledge enables him to predict, not as a good one, who finds his reasons for conduct, whether inside the law or outside of it, in the vaguer sanctions of conscience."[6] While the goal of tort reform needn't be making "citizens into angels," neither can it afford merely to impose itself when reform, alone, will be ineffective.[7] "Knowing" the law as will serve to improve a society requires understanding where the efficacy of law leaves off and where the efficacy of still other public institutions begins.

Unaffordability with labor plays an important role in changing the American sense of offense, moving that sense from one measured by objective loss, including economic, to one that is directly proportional to the wealth of the offender. I stand with tort-reformers on this particular fact: the contemporary American seems able to suffer through nearly any offensive action by a poor person because the person is poor and cannot pay anything even if found guilty. If the same offensive action was committed by a rich person, however slight, the same victim is likely to allege that he has a suffered total and permanent nervous breakdown and that all manner of tortuous harm has come upon his entire family, as well.

There is limited justification for this rule of proportionality. When a person is legitimately wronged by another who is judgment-proof, it is foolish to undertake costly litigation unless it is to vindicate a moral principle. If payoff is all one seeks, it is a waste of time to bring a civil tort of wrongful death against the down-and-out drunkard who runs down a loved one. In such cases the suit will nearly always be brought, however, because the memory of the loved one insists. Similarly, for a marginal harm that will not bankrupt one morally or economically, it makes sense to sue an offender who can and should absorb the debt.

What bends reason is bringing suit for a marginal harm as if to, and for amounts of damages designed to, vindicate a moral principle. For example, employers have come to expect lawsuits for terminating any employee, even the most incompetent and misbehaved of them. In bringing such claims, workers typically allege only trivial damages for lost wages, but they deserve hundreds of thousands of dollars—not uncommonly millions—for the "emotional distress" of being told they must find work elsewhere.

Being fired is rarely a medically traumatic event. And, even when wrong, employers believe they have just cause for termination; that is, they have tried to act in good faith. But worse, the litigation of such cases often reveals that such employees never saw a doctor or displayed emotional instability to friends or family; that they continued on with their normal activities, including the celebratory ones; and that the employees had no reason at all for thinking that the employer acted in bad faith as could warrant damages intended to punish the employer as opposed to simply making the employee whole.

This cultural misjudgment prevails in the United States, and it is not one that tort reform laws can fix. Likewise, removing the seduction of large damage awards may moderate attorneys' temptation to undertake litigation of unworthy claims from knowledge that certain classes of cases will never reach the stage of actual adjudication. It will have no affect whatsoever on the temptation of the affronted laborer to sue for profit, however, because his is a moral cause and also because he will settle for so little relative to the costs of litigation and call it a genuine victory.

Here is the punch line on tort reform laws. If the attractiveness of large damage awards is grounded in Americans' distrust that their own labor is sufficient to afford items of decency, then lawsuit abuse is merely a symptom of a deeper problem rather than a cause itself. In that case, tort reforms laws are remarkably shortsighted. Even if implemented with full success, the approach merely demands that Americans find new means of grifting.

As explained above, this solution may satisfy those whose main concern is purging the legal process of certain misuses. As a societal problem, this solution will not do, however. Overlitigiousness interpreted as a national character defect will manifest itself in a multitude of ways. As long as this kind of disrespect for law is grounded in widespread economic frustration, it will almost certainly lead to other legally and ethically questionable conduct, which may be more harmful and costly to society than lawsuit abuse.

> *A Lottery is a Taxation,*
> *Upon all the Fools in Creation;*
> *It is easily rais'd,*
> *Credulity always in Fashion;*
> *For, Folly's a Fund,*
> *Will never lose Ground;*
> *While Fools are so rife in the Nation.*
> —Henry Fielding, *The Lottery*

The idea that unaffordability with labor has unappreciated social costs is bolstered by the observation that disproportionate numbers of poor persons participate in state lotteries, gambling proportionately higher amounts of their earnings and suffering pathological problems more frequently. The National Gambling Impact Study Commission found that in 1997, although people at all points on the income spectrum played the lottery, players with household incomes under $10,000 spent almost three time as much money on lotteries as those with incomes over $50,000. Not only did the poorest participants spend a higher percentage of their incomes on the lottery, but they also spent more as a dollar amount. Those with household incomes under $10,000 spent more per capita ($597) than those with incomes from $10,000–$24,999 ($569) and considerably more than those with incomes of $25,000–$49,999 ($382), $50,000–$99,999 ($225), and over $100,000 ($196).[8]

The NGISC research has been repeatedly affirmed, including in the findings of states from research into their own lotteries.[9] In an attempt to prevent the adoption of a state lottery, the Alabama Policy Institute produced a report purporting to examine the dark side of public lotteries in other states. For my purposes, the most relevant findings of the Alabama study are these: the less educated people are, the more likely they will gamble heavily; the less money people earn per year, the more likely they will become pathological gamblers; and "whereas the affluent tend to view the lottery as entertainment and as a source of increased spending on products and services important to higher-income households, the poor see it as a way to escape the drudgery of uninteresting, routine work and improve their living standards."[10]

At the end of the day, however compelling, statistics about the correlations between gambling and poverty and gambling and being uneducated cannot prove as a matter of social psychology that unaffordability with labor is a source driving people to tithe to state lotteries. For that, we must boldly rely on our own common sense. I, for one, am convinced that many who tithe to the state lotteries are so drawn to them not as low-stakes forms of recreation but in hopes of an economic salvation they believe is not to be found—certainly not through hard work. The draw of the poor toward state lotteries and other forms of gambling is living proof of many Americans' low estimation of their ability to earn.

An important obstacle to empathizing with lawsuit and lottery abusers, whether they are motivated by the indignity of unaffordability or other reasons, is the fact that their conduct is arguably voluntary. Both face a near-irrebuttable presumption that they alone bear responsibility for their dysfunction. This may be correct, but see it through.

Americans continue to believe categorically in individual responsibility. They exhibit little tolerance or respect for fine moral distinctions, insisting instead upon clear lines in the sand. When asked upon whom responsibility should fall for the consequences of some new social development, the American answer is never "here, but" or "there, except." It is either fully one's responsibility or fully another's responsibility; either it is completely your fault or completely my fault. Even when the truth of the matter is grey, the answers to such questions are often as clear in the American mind as black and white.

There is also very little discord among Americans regarding the domain of individual responsibility and its limits. By consensus, even among citizens who stand to be burdened by new affirmations of individual responsibility, such questions are routinely resolved in favor of freedom rather than disposition or determination. Americans know that each concession to disposition or determination shrinks considerably the palpable province of freedom. Each admission of a new disability is an admission that human beings are altogether less free. From this recognition, Americans have developed the habit of erring on the side of free choice. In moments of doubt, Americans prefer to feign freedom rather than grapple with its true dimensions.

On the whole, Americans' enlightened ignorance on the subject of freedom is an indispensable virtue. One consequence of such a strong presumption of freedom, however, is that Americans tend to ignore conduct indicative of a social problem unless it can be characterized as environmentally caused rather than individually chosen. Individually destructive conduct that may be better understood in light of surrounding social hardships, such as habitually abusing dangerous drugs or gambling away one's paycheck, is often interpreted merely as poor personal choice. Such conduct usually is chosen and is, indeed, poor choosing. But it is the full nature of the social hardship with which the destructive conduct is correlated, not just the degree of freedom underlying the choices, that should dictate the nation's concern.

To the extent that it signals the disintegration of the possibility of labor-based economic stability in America, the facts of lawsuit and lottery abuse are nationally important whether or not the conduct is fully the product of free wills.

NOTES

1. In 2006 in West Virginia, a mining accident occurred that resulted in the deaths of twelve of thirteen miners. Due to a lack of communication, the families standing by for news of their loved ones were mistakenly told that

twelve of the thirteen miners *had survived*. Needless to say, the correction was a painful one. Upon learning the truth of the situation a grieving family member is reported to have said, "I call this an injustice. I can tell you this much. I am going to sue." The family member recanted upon learning that the rumor began with an excited utterance by a rescue worker who found the one surviving miner before discovering that the rest had died, but the initial reaction is its own proof.

2. In 2005, shortly after Hurricane Katrina, I came across several newspaper articles reporting that a victim of the storm had won the lottery. According to the stories, the person hit the jackpot just a few weeks after the storm. Like many who suffered that catastrophe, the woman apparently had lost her living as well as her place to live. At the time I recall being surprised at the victorious "man-over-nature" tone of the news stories when the question that stick in my mind was "Why was a person in those circumstances gambling at all?" I now believe this story to be an urban myth, as I've not been able to identify the sources that first brought it to my attention. However, the story is a familiar one to many Americans, and one need only visit the nearest casino to see the unpleasant truth in this fable.

3. See, e.g., Mark Browne and Robert Puelz, "The Effect of Legal Rules on the Value of Economic and Non-economic Damages and the Decision to File," *Journal of Risk and Uncertainty* 18, no. 2 (August 1999): 189–213. However, a 2005 study found that 96 percent of all medical malpractice cases settle and that for the 4 percent of claims that go to trial, the average side of damage awards grew only 3.4 percent between 1991 and 2003. Thus, in 1991 medical malpractice payments accounted for about $10 of every $1,000 spent on physician and clinical services. In 2002, after adjusting for inflation, medical malpractice payments accounted for only $12 of every $1,000 spent on physician and clinical services. Even more striking, the study found that for the period in question, medical malpractice payments grew at roughly the same rate as healthcare costs overall. Amitabh Chandra, Shantanu Nundy, and Seth Seabury, "The Growth of Physician Medical Malpractice Payments: Evidence from the National Practitioner Databank" *Health Affairs*, May 2005, http://content.healthaffairs.org/cgi/content/abstract/hlthaff.w5.240 (accessed September 20, 2006).

4. John J. Donahue III and Peter Siegelman, "The Changing Nature of Employment Discrimination Litigation," *Stanford Law Review* 43 (1991): 983, 990.

5. John J. Donahue III and Peter Siegelman, "The Evolution of Employment Discrimination Law in the 1990s: A Preliminary Investigation," in *The Handbook of Employment Discrimination Research: Rights and Realities*, ed. Laura B. Nelson and Robert L. Nelson, 282–83 (The Netherlands: Springer, 2005).

6. Oliver Wendell Holmes Jr., "The Path of the Law," *Harvard Law Review* 10, no. 457 (1897).

7. In *The Federalist Papers*, no. 51, James Madison famously writes, "If men were angels, no government would be necessary. If angels were to govern men, neither external nor internal controls on government would be necessary."

8. "National Gambling Impact Study Commission Final Report, Executive Summary" (1999), as reported in Alicia Hanson, "Lotteries and State Fiscal Policy," *Tax Foundation Background Paper* no. 46 (October 2004): 28. Hanson observes that one study found a small but positive relationship between unemployment rates and lottery ticket sales, suggesting that some may view the lottery as a solution to financial hardship, spending money on it when they can least afford it.

9. See, e.g., Joseph McCrary and Thomas Pavlak, "Who Plays the Georgia Lottery? Results of a Statewide Survey," Public Policy Research Series, Carl Vinson Institute of Government, University of Georgia (2002): 12.

10. Alabama Policy Institute, "An Alabama Lottery: Theft by Consent," institute report, 2002, p. 17.

CHAPTER 2
Traditionalism and the Rise of the Credit Welfare System

One of the technical means which the modern employer uses in order to secure the greatest possible amount of work from his men is the device of piece rates.... But a peculiar difficulty has been met with surprising frequency: raising the piece rates has often had the result that not more but less has been accomplished in the same time, because the worker reacted to the increase not by increasing but by decreasing the amount of his work. A man, for instance, who at the rate of 1 mark per acre mowed 2½ acres per day and earned 2½ marks, when the rate was raised to 1.25 marks per acre mowed, not 3 acres, as might be easily have done, thus earning 3.75 marks, but only 2 acres, so that he could still earn the 2½ marks to which he was accustomed. The opportunity of earning more was less attractive than that of working less. He did not ask: "how much can I earn in a day if I do as much work as possible?," but: how much must I work in order to cam the wage, 2½ marks, which I earned before and which takes care of my traditional needs? This is what is here meant by "traditionalism." A man does not "by nature" wish to cam more and more money, but simply to live as he is accustomed to live and to earn as much as is necessary for that purpose.
—Max Weber, *The Protestant Ethic and the Spirit of Capitalism*

The great increase in consumer indebtedness in our time has been widely viewed as reflecting some original or unique change in popular attitudes or behavior. People have changed their view of debt. Thus there has been an inexplicable but very real retreat from the Puritan canon that required an individual to save first and enjoy later. In fact, as always, the pieces of economic life are part of the whole. It would be surprising indeed if a society that is prepared to spend thousands of millions to persuade people of their wants were to fail to take the further step of financing these wants, and were it not then to go on to persuade people of the ease and desirability of incurring debt to make these wants effective. This has happened. The process of persuading people to incur debt, and the arrangements for them to do so, are as much a part of modern production as the making of the goods and the nurturing of the wants. The Puritan ethos was not abandoned. It was merely overwhelmed by the massive power of modern merchandising.

—John Kenneth Galbraith, *The Affluent Society*

Weber claims that, in free market economies, a person's natural tendency is to work only as much as needed to meet his or her traditional needs, and that special incentives are required to bring persons to want to and to be willing to work additional hours for nontraditional products. This, as Galbraith explains, is the main purpose of commercial advertising—to create consumer desires of such strength that certain products feel necessary to have—so necessary that borrowing more and more money becomes a permanent feature of daily life. Whenever these nontraditional products receive the customary status of items of decency, they become tied to one's dignity and community standing. But supposing that American commercialism long ago succeeded in shaking Americans from any traditionalism, making them desirous of more money with which to purchase things on impulse, Weber assumes that we will accomplish this higher standard of living mainly by working more. He does not explore the possibility that citizens might accomplish the higher standard of living by other means, such as credit, thereby enabling for a time the ability to afford a higher standard of living with the same amount of work.

The indignity of unaffordability exacts a price here. When items of decency prove unaffordable through labor but credit is readily available, credit may become a permanent source of supplemental income—a private welfare system of sorts—used to *borrow* items of decency and the dignity that comes along with them. One side effect of using credit as private welfare, of course, is substantial indebtedness, which itself is (or at least used to be) a source of character suspicion in America.

The fact that Americans are increasingly willing to accept relatively permanent indebtedness in order to afford items of decency not obtainable through their labor is a remarkable sociological development. The Protestant work ethic that Weber demonstrated to hold true in America and that raises work from a mere necessity of survival to the level of individual calling derives much of its value from its role in achieving economic independence, understood here as the absence of indebtedness to others. The comfort of contemporary Americans with extreme borrowing may be interpreted as the relinquishment of the goal of economic independence through hard work alone and as an acceptance that a decent life today is often possible only through private or public subsidization. Having accepted that hard work is no longer sufficient to obtain items of decency, the part of this morality claiming that to be good, one had to be economically independent, is no longer pertinent and so has been discarded.

The American conception of economic responsibility is driven by romantic images and stories of a past America, be they real or imagined, in which nearly every American exhibited the following economic virtues. First and foremost, historically, Americans took great pride in making their own way. Not looking to government or private charity and being left alone to stand and fall by one's own decisions and effort were considered birthrights. Second, because making one's own way was central to one's dignity, Americans happily made due with whatever they had. Only in the direst of circumstances would Americans even consider seeking public or private assistance. The decision to ask another for help was a momentous occasion.

Third, Americans saved rather than borrowed to obtain items they could not immediately afford. For them, the very idea of indebtedness to another—whether to a government, bank, church, or relative—was inherently distasteful, because "owing" offended their sense of freedom. Fourth, Americans controlled urges to measure their success purely in economic terms or according to how much others had; they held in check their desires to keep up with the Joneses. Fifth and finally, Americans were adept at distinguishing necessity from nicety, and in lean times their ability to delay gratification saw them through.

Historian Lendol Calder describes this strand of American romanticism as "the myth of lost economic virtue," whose origins he traces as far back as Mark Twain's first novel, *The Gilded Age*.[1] Calder describes this American conception of economic responsibility as mythical because his own research reveals consumer credit debt to be a rather constant historical reality. In his own words: "A river of red ink runs through American history." For better or worse, it is this account of economic responsibility to which Americans turn when evaluating the public concern over private indebtedness. The irony is that to the extent one adopts this model of economic responsibility, personal indebtedness will not appear to be of public concern. To the contrary, this account of economic responsibility casts Americans' indebtedness as a wholly private undertaking—all private contracts and arm's length dealings between sufficiently sophisticated bargainers.

My own objection to this romantic historical view of economic responsibility is that it focuses almost exclusively upon the conduct of debtors, for the most part placing above suspicion the conduct of creditors. If the debtor can be shown to have a rudimentary understanding of the terms of the agreement as disclosed by the creditor, the inquiry into the creditor's behavior is at an end. In that case, the obligations of credit institutions begin and end with disclosure (and, of course, honoring the terms of the bargain). Under such a view there cannot be such things as predatory lending or usury—the charging of often-exorbitant interest rates—or other forms of exploitation alongside disclosure, except when debtors are judged to be incapable of understanding the terms of the agreements they entered into.

Applying this conception of economic responsibility to disconcerting data about personal indebtedness and individual bankruptcy, the conclusion is not surprising: if individual bankruptcies and debt loads are increasing, then contemporary Americans must be more economically irresponsible than their more virtuous forefathers and foremothers, real or imagined.

Outstanding debts for consumer credit totaled more than $2.1 trillion in 2005, which averages out to be a little more than $9,700 worth of outstanding credit for each American above the age of eighteen. Economists disagree over whether this is necessarily a bad development and, if so, whether it is necessarily a critically bad development. The general public, on the other hand, has taken a decidedly negative view of the matter. In an analysis of patterns of consumer debt, journalists Thomas Durkin and Zachariah Jonasson reported that of all the relevant articles printed in the *New York Times* from 1965 to 1995, 69 percent were negative in tone.[2] That is explained, I submit, by the fact that according to the American conception of economic responsibility, it is nearly always a bad thing to be economically indebted and always a critically bad thing to be deeply economically indebted. Furthermore, in a culture adhering to the outmoded view that creditors fully meet their obligations simply through disclosure, the American conception of economic responsibility lays any blame at debtors' feet. Largely through ignorance of the possibility of *exploitation notwithstanding disclosure*, creditors receive a moral pass.

According to the US Courts Bankruptcy Statistics, 2005 yielded 2,078,415 individual (nonbusiness) bankruptcies, up from 1,597,462 in 2004, a 30.5 percent increase in bankruptcies in a twelve month period. Interpreting the moral significance of bankruptcy filings is difficult. An increase in the raw number of filings is likely due to multiple factors not easily separated out. For example, such numbers do not clearly indicate economic irresponsibility or insurmountable economic hardship, or any particular correlation between the two. Such numbers in the future will also be affected by the prevailing bankruptcy regime, as set by Congress and administered by US bankruptcy courts, which can expand or contract the pool of individuals considered eligible for bankruptcy filing for a given period. For example, part of the 2004–2005 increase in individual bankruptcy filings is undoubtedly attributable to individuals seeking to file prior to changes in bankruptcy rules implemented in 2005, which, among other things, placed new restrictions on certain discharges and exemptions. Nonetheless, the American conception of economic responsibility colors such statistics against debtors and in favor of creditors, supporting the conclusion that increases in the number of individual bankruptcies is somehow evidence of raw increases in economic irresponsibility.

Americans' historical derision of indebtedness and bankruptcy has obvious flaws. On its face, at least, it fails to account for the many forms of "good debt" for which the returns on borrowing exceed the costs of financing the same; in some cases, increasing access to bankruptcy can stimulate the economy. For example, a major function of bankruptcy filings under Chapter 11 of the US Bankruptcy Code enables financially troubled companies to reorganize for purposes of remaining in business and to negotiate with creditors who might otherwise sink the business by demanding payments all at once.

What I have called the American conception of economic responsibility probably also retains vestiges of an inherited Christian understanding of the moral significance of indebtedness. Elizabeth Anderson, philosopher and author of *Value in Ethics and Economics*, writes, "Within the Christian ethic, credit had long been a morally perilous situation. For centuries, the Catholic Church had prohibited, on Biblical authority (Deut. 23:19), the charging of interest among Christians. The task of doing so was assigned to Jews, who were thereby constituted as social pariahs. Although the Protestant Reformation had relaxed the rules against interest, and interest had become indispensable to the transatlantic economy, the granting of loans among Christians without interest was still commonplace. By the 18th century, the main moral onus of credit rested with debtors. Indebtedness carried a moral taint, suggesting profligacy and vanity. Failure to pay off one's debts was a sin. Debtors in default could be bound over in service to their creditors, or thrown into debtors' prison. These punishments were widely mentioned in the Bible (e.g., 2 Kings 4:1; Matthew 18:25), and widely practiced in Europe and the Americas."[3]

But whatever the flaws of the traditional American attitude toward indebtedness, contemporary Americans are legitimately critical of the supposition that creditors' obligations end with full disclosure of their practices and policies in fine print. Perhaps this was a sound model of creditor-debtor relations in an earlier, simpler America. Today, however, exploitation with disclosure, or its modern-day, hyper-technical counterpart, is not only possible, but it is arguably already rampant.

From the complexity of credit arrangements, many people have already concluded that new reforms are required in order to ensure that borrowers engage the credit welfare system with their eyes wide open. For example, Democratic Senator Chris Dodd of Connecticut, a member of the US Senate's Banking Committee, has tried numerous times to get legislation passed that would change the practices of the credit card industry. While such reforms are necessary in any case because the conduct of credit card issuers is so ethically suspect, they ultimately fail to reach the heart of the matter. As explained below, given the current indispensability of the credit welfare system to items of decency, Americans will continue to rely upon it as supplemental income despite full disclosure of the risks.

The plain fact is that interest payments account for more than 80 percent of the profits of credit card issuers, with the remaining 20 percent coming from annual fees, late fees, over-limit fees, and merchant fees. The enormous profits available from people who charge up to the limits and pay only the minimum each month have made delinquent card holders who pay high interest the most valued customers in the business. "Subprime lending," granting credit specifically to people who are living on the edge, is a large new niche in the credit

business, and one much applauded on Wall Street.... The credit card companies hope to expand credit card debt even further.... Their most aggressive targeting is aimed at the only group left that is not already inundated with plastic: the poor. In a marketing push that they euphemistically refer to as the "democratization of credit," credit card lenders have pressed their credit cards on people they shunned only a few years ago. Such "democratization" means that more poor people will be able to spend their way into middle-class consumption at 18 percent interest. The results of the industry's extraordinary marketing efforts have paid off. Credit card usage has grown fastest in recent years among debtors with the lowest incomes. Since the early 1990s, Americans with incomes below the poverty level nearly doubled their credit card usage, and those in the $10,000–25,000 income bracket come in a close second in their rise in debt. The result is not surprising: 27 percent of the under-$10,000 families have consumer debt that is more than 40 percent of their income, and nearly one in ten has at least one debt that is more than sixty days past due.[4]

—Teresa A. Sullivan, Elizabeth Warren, and Jay Lawrence Westbrook,
The Fragile Middle Class: Americans in Debt

Some would argue that there is absolutely nothing morally wrong with the above fact pattern, relying upon two alleged, deceptively simple facts: *first*, no adult person, whatever his or her income bracket, is forced to accept an offer of credit on any terms he or she finds disagreeable; *second*, any adult person's acceptance of an offer of credit implies that such terms were, in fact, agreeable. This raises a very old philosophical debate, started, and in some important respects finished in the eighteenth century, by Jeremy Bentham in his *Defence of Usury*.[5]

There, Bentham presents a moral defense of the "democratization of credit," including the view that there can be no such thing as unfair credit practices alongside disclosure: "My neighbors, being at liberty, have happened to concur among themselves in dealing at a certain rate of interest," Bentham writes. "I, who have money to lend, and Titius, who wants to borrow it of me, would be glad, the one of us to accept, the other to give, an interest somewhat higher than theirs: why is the liberty they exercise to be made a pretence for depriving me and Titius of ours?"

The major contribution of Bentham's work is the observation that any regulation of interest rates that may be charged by lenders and creditors freely transacting must be grounded in social custom rather than any objective truth of the matter. For Bentham, interest rates have nothing to do with morality, or right or wrong:

> One thing then is plain; that, antecedently to custom growing from convention, there can be no such thing as usury: for what rate of interest is there that can naturally be more proper than another? What natural fixed price can there be for the use of money more than for the use of any other thing? Were it not then for custom, usury, considered in a moral view, would not then so much as admit of a definition: so far from having an existence, it would not be so much as conceivable: nor therefore could the law, in the definition it took upon itself to give of such offence, have so much as a guide to steer by. Custom therefore is the sole basis, which, either the moralist in his rules and precepts, or the legislator in his injunctions, can have to build upon.

Supposing Bentham is right, the same is true of all manner of morals-based legislation that many Americans support, from the prohibition of abortion to the use of controlled substances, plural and gay marriages, stem-cell research, and euthanasia, most of which appeal to social custom as justification. This does not detract from the validity of Bentham's position, however, provided one is prepared to attack social custom as a basis for policy wherever it rears its purportedly ugly head. On the other hand, this argument will not go very far when presented to Americans who are strong supporters of tradition; for them, custom remains a trustworthy basis for directing at least some legal affairs, such as those connected with religious belief. In that case, social custom may very well be suitable for assessing at what point and in which contexts rates of interest qualify as too high, or as highway robbery, in *this* nation.[6]

Bentham's anecdotal example of a free transaction between he and Titius is compelling as applied to some contemporary uses of credit, such as the adjustable rate mortgage. The adjustable rate mortgage is an innovation that has enabled a great many Americans to obtain home loans that they otherwise could not qualify for. In and of itself, the innovation that is the adjustable rate mortgage does not seem morally suspect or suggest that people who opt for such credit arrangements are incapable of appreciating the nature of the risks that may materialize. But, if extended too far—such as to persons whose financial backgrounds contain little or no evidence of an ability to maintain a mortgage, or whose qualification depends upon their never suffering any financial setbacks—the adjustable rate mortgage is transformed into so much snake oil. And, right now, it is becoming apparent that the subprime lending industry—an industry based upon loans to individuals who could not obtain credit on normal terms because their credit histories are either very poor or nonexistent—is replete with snake oil salesmen. Many of those companies made millions on subprime loans, especially during the last decade, but then declared bankruptcy alongside record foreclosures upon the homes of the borrowers that they unscrupulously lent money to.

The authors of *The Fragile Middle Class* have shown that many credit card issuers are just this kind of snake oil salesmen. For many of them, the democratization of credit does not mean finding innovative ways to extend credit to persons using a more liberal but still sound definition of "creditworthiness." Rather, it means extending credit to people who are notably *not* creditworthy by any plausible definition. They hope that borrowers will routinely fail to timely pay their debts and, for issuers, default is not an entirely unwelcome development. Morally speaking, this approach to "democratizing" credit is unsavory for the same reasons that loan-sharking is, absent the shattering of kneecaps in dark alleyways.

But Bentham's argument still stands: there is nothing about being a low-income person that necessarily renders one incapable of appreciating the risks of accepting credit card offers, however usurious the terms. We must also address the huge numbers of well-educated, middle-class Americans for whom credit cards have become a permanent source of private welfare.

The key assumption in Bentham's argument in defense of usury is that both parties, lender and borrower—Citibank, American Express, Chase Manhattan, Discover, FleetBoston, MasterCard, Bank of America, Visa, *and you*—are fully and equally "at liberty" to transact. Ultimately, I agree with Bentham. But the fact that contemporary Americans live out their entire lives immersed in consumer advertising with synthetic druglike efficacy and that they are ever more desperate to secure the full complement of items of decency is not irrelevant to the conclusion. Rather, taking full account of these factors, the argument that Americans are fully at liberty when they use credit as private welfare follows a more circuitous and unsettling route. That route begins with understanding how the complexity of modern business has changed both the nature and the mechanisms of disclosure.

Disclosure serves two very different purposes: first, to put in writing the essential terms of the bargain, including disclosure of the risks, and second, to comply with a substantial body of federal and state regulation, the violations of which can result in costly legal actions. The first purpose of disclosure is most important to borrowers, and the second is most important to lenders. A recent episode of PBS's documentary news show *Frontline*, titled "The Secret History of the Credit Card," carries these two concerns about disclosure and Bentham's arguments about transacting at liberty into the twenty-first century. There, coauthor of *The Fragile Middle Class* Elizabeth Warren argues that fair agreements with the credit card industry are impossible for two reasons.

First, because credit card issuers are permitted to change the terms of the contract at any time, for virtually any reason, there really are no firm contractual obligations on the part of credit card issuers but only duties for the credit card holders to pay whenever and whatever the issuer deems appropriate. On this argument, credit card issuers appear more like loan sharks even than suggested earlier, as they reserve the right to up the interest ante by whim or caprice, with government lying in wait to break financial knees, no questions asked.

Second, in addition to the imbalance of bargaining power between lenders and borrowers, credit card issuers further undermine the liberty of individuals by withholding information vital to informed consent, such as showing on a statement how long it would take for a person to expunge his debt if he only made the minimum payments. According to Warren, credit card issuers resist the simple inclusion of a sentence stating, "If cardholder makes minimum payments, it will take x years and y months to repay the debt," perhaps because such information promises a fuller apprehension of the impact of minimum credit card payments upon a long-term borrower's financial prospects.

In opposition to this view, financial wizard Andrew Kahr contends that the additional disclosure Warren recommends would be useless, as consumers are not interested in such information and do not consider it essential to the determination of whether or not they will accept the terms of credit card offers. In the *Frontline* episode, Kahr's opinion is likely carelessly offered, for it is possible for a person not to want to know certain information before entering into a contract *although* that information is essential to making an informed decision. This is especially true of agreements as counterintuitive as credit card contracts. Indeed, one reason corporations generally carry greater disclosure obligations is because they can be expected to know of certain particulars, such as universal default provisions, which permit credit card companies to increases an individual's interest rate for failing to make timely payments to *other* creditors. Average consumers cannot fairly be expected to know about these particulars.

Kahr's claim that disclosure of such information is useless because consumers do not ask for it is likelier evidence that consumers are not aware that such information is pertinent to their decisions, or that such terms will apply to their agreements at all. In any case, the obligation to disclose the material terms of a bargain is not based upon what the other party intends to do with the information, but it has only to do with ensuring that formation of the contract is not flawed by one party withholding relevant data. If Warren is correct, such data are relevant as a means of explaining to unsophisticated and poorly leveraged borrowers the full import of their signatures on the dotted line, a claim that Kahr, if consulted further, may or may not dispute.

There is independent data to support Warren's position. The United States Office of the Comptroller of the Currency (OCC) charters, regulates, and supervises all national banks and supervises the federal branches and agencies of foreign banks. In 2004 the OCC issued an advisory letter "to alert national banks to its concerns regarding certain credit card marketing and account management practices." The alert raised concerns about three practices: One, soliciting for credit cards that advertise credit limits "up to" a maximum dollar amount when that credit limit is, in fact, seldom extended; two, using promotional rates in credit card solicitations without clearly disclosing the significant restrictions on the applicability of those rates; and three, increasing a cardholder's annual percentage rate or otherwise increasing a cardholder's cost of credit when the circumstances triggering the increase, or the creditor's right to effectuate the increase, have not been fully or prominently disclosed.[7]

As to the third concern, addressed under the heading "Repricing of Accounts and Other Changes in Credit Terms," the letter states:

Credit card issuers may increase a consumer's APR [annual percentage rate] to address credit risks that arise when a consumer fails to make timely payments on the account, and some credit card issuers may increase the APR when a consumer fails to make timely payments on <u>other</u> accounts, including accounts with other creditors. Some credit card issuers also may raise a consumer's APR for other reasons, such as the consumer's increased use of credit, failure to make more than the minimum monthly payment on the account with the issuer, or other behavior that reflects adversely on the consumer's credit rating. Credit card issuers may take other actions that also effectively increase the cost of credit for some consumers, such as shortening the due date for receipt of payment or raising the amount of fees for late payment, exceeding a credit limit, or obtaining a cash advance.

These practices may well be appropriate measures for managing credit risk on the part of the credit card issuer. However, certain practices in connection with repricing credit card accounts and changing terms of credit card agreements may raise heightened compliance and reputation risks. Accordingly, national banks should not:

- Fail to disclose fully and prominently in promotional materials the circumstances under which the credit card agreement permits the bank to increase the consumer's APR (other than due to a variable rate feature), increase fees, or take other action to increase the cost of credit, such as, if applicable, failure to make timely payments to *another* creditor.
- Fail to disclose fully and prominently in marketing materials and credit agreements, as applicable, that the bank reserves the right to change the APR (other than due to a variable rate feature), fees, or other credit terms unilaterally.

In other words, à la Bentham, the US government's official position is that disclosure is the beginning and the end of obligations for the credit card industry. As weak as such regulations are—it is difficult to imagine what the credit card industry has to object to regarding the above—the OCC missive does not refer to any legal sanctions for failure to comply with such minimal restrictions, or how seriously such violations will be regarded or investigated, if at all. As the regulatory agency charged with ensuring the ethical conduct of the credit card industry, the above advisory letter is persuasive evidence that Warren is correct about the one-sided, adhesive nature of current credit card agreements.

Nonetheless, Warren's argument ultimately fails to answer Bentham's contention that Americans who enter into credit card agreements for private welfare purposes remain fully at liberty to do so. To return to the line of thought at the beginning of this chapter, Americans are presently driven by the desire to borrow more and more money because, even with reputable labor, additional resources are often needed to obtain items of decency. Legislation correcting the credit card industry's poor disclosure practices, while necessary as a matter of good law and plain justice, will not quench such personal desires. That is, the desire to live decently, by virtually any means, will in most cases override whatever repellent effect is gained by forcing Americans to confront, before signing, the full binding burden of credit card agreements. That is why even more insidious arrangements than those offered by the credit card industry, such as payday loans (usury if it ever was), are also in great demand.

To return to Galbraith, "the massive power of merchandising" has so overwhelmed the Puritan ethos that counseled Americans to save first and enjoy later, that apparently even the credit card industry cannot fathom it. The resistance of the credit card industry to making clearer disclosures, such as incorporating into billing statements repayment time lines based on a borrower's payment practices, is wholly misplaced. Fuller disclosure will not cause Americans to depend less upon credit as private welfare. This, I suspect, was Kahr's true message, or the overriding truth buried within it.

Bentham and the credit card industry win in spite of themselves, and not due to the confusion created by improper disclosure of the terms by which they extend credit. Rather, with the eradication of traditionalism and replacement of it with the credit welfare system, even the fullest, most crude and scary disclosures will not dissuade people from accepting credit under the most discreditable of terms, wherever deemed necessary to obtains items of decency that, right now, cannot be provided through reasonable amounts of their labor.

Some may argue that the true solution to Americans' unhealthy reliance upon credit, which mass marketing continues effectively to forestall, is the individual moderation of desire—the choice to want much, much less. Of the need for such economic moderation, Thoreau eloquently wrote:

> Perhaps I am more than usually jealous with respect to my freedom. . . . Those slight labors which afford me a livelihood, and by which it is allowed that I am to some extent serviceable to my contemporaries, are as yet commonly a pleasure to me, and I am not often reminded that they are a necessity. So far I am successful. But I foresee that if my wants should be much increased, the labor required to supply them would become a drudgery. If I should sell both my forenoons and afternoons to society, as most appear to do, I am sure that for me there would be nothing worth living for. I trust that I shall never thus sell my birthright for a mess of pottage. . . . But as it is said of the merchants that ninety-seven in a hundred fail, so the life of men generally, tried by this standard, is a failure, and bankruptcy may be surely prophesied.[8]

But what should Americans want less of? To the extent that Thoreau and others claim that Americans should want less items of decency—less desire for basic healthcare, less desire to own a home, less desire to send one's children to good schools, less desire for a reliable vehicle, less desire for a good linen shirt and good pair of leather shoes—the criticisms miss the mark. Asking Americans to want less of these things is akin to asking them to accept, and to be unaffected by, the indignity of unaffordability.

It is also to admonish them for wishing to belong to mainstream America. Americans are already acclimated, or maybe resigned, to the facts that they must sell both their forenoons and afternoons to society in order to earn a decent living. They have also accepted the "drudgery" of working full-time for a lifetime and, by and large, they do not complain about the shrinking slices of life that remain when work is over. Their acceptance of these conditions is from recognition that earning a traditional, decent American life is worth the sacrifice.

But many Americans have reached the point where the amounts of labor needed simply to afford items of decency leaves no room whatsoever for actually living. The inability of many Americans to make anything of their nonworking lives—because the hourly economic rewards of their working lives is so inadequate—forces Thoreau's fateful choice: shall they simply accept that a traditional, decent American life is not possible for them, or should they borrow the money needed to buy one, at least until their luck runs out?

Faced with this kind of choice, some kind of bankruptcy—economic or moral, perhaps both—is predictable. For those who cannot afford to repay the credit they obtain, the credit itself is a time bomb that will eventually explode, causing even greater financial difficulties than their pre-credit days. This is what has happened in the subprime home loan market, leaving many Americans facing foreclosure upon their homes due to the materialization of risks that they could not possibly have prepared for.[9]

Even more damaging, however, is having to accept the reality that hard work is not the savior of America; that is, that in this America, a decent life is increasingly beyond an individual's control.

NOTES

1. Lendol Calder, *Financing the American Dream: A Cultural History of Consumer Credit* (Princeton, NJ: Princeton University Press, 1999), pp. 23–26.

2. Thomas Durkin and Zachariah Jonasson, "An Empirical Evaluation of the Content and Cycle of Financial Reporting: The Case of Consumer Credit," Credit Research Center Working Paper 64 (April 2002): 20.

3. Elizabeth Anderson, "Ethical Assumptions in Economic Theory: Some Lessons from the History of Credit and Bankruptcy," *Ethical Theory and Moral Practice* 7 (July 2004): 348.

4. Teresa A. Sullivan, Elizabeth Warren, and Jay Lawrence Westbrook, *The Fragile Middle Class: Americans in Debt* (New Haven, CT: Yale University Press, 2000), pp. 135–37 (internal citations omitted).

5. Jeremy Bentham, *Defence of Usury: Shewing the Impolicy of the*

Present Legal Restraints on the Terms of Pecuniary Bargains; In Letters to a Friend to Which Is Added a Letter to Adam Smith, Esq. LL.D.; On the Discouragements Opposed by the above Restraints to the Progress of Inventive Industry, Letter 2, part 4 (1816), available online at the Library of Economics and Liberty, http://www.econlib.org/LIBRARY/Bentham/bnthUs.html (accessed September 20, 2006).

6. *Marquette National Bank v. First of Omaha Service Corp.*, 439 U.S. 299 (1978) allowed national banks to charge interest "at the rate allowed by the laws of the State . . . where the bank is located." As a result, eight of the ten largest credit card issuers with national charters now reside in states with no interest rate caps—that is, states with no prohibitions on anything that Americans might consider usury. The other two banks are in Arizona, which caps the interest rates that banks may charge at 36 percent.

7. OCC advisory letter, AL 2004-10, September 14, 2004.

8. Henry David Thoreau, "Life without Principle," in *Walden and Other Writings* (New York: Barnes & Noble Books, 1993), p. 353.

9. While preparing this book for publication, in March 2007 news organizations were reporting that more than two million Americans with subprime loans were facing foreclosure on their homes in 2007, and nearly 20 percent of subprime mortgages issued between 2005 and 2006 were projected to fail. This was according to a December 2006 report by the Center for Responsible Lending, a nonpartisan research and policy organization. Senate Banking Committee Chairman Christopher Dodd (D-CT), head of the investigation looking into the matter, referred to the home loan industry's practices as "unconscionable and deceptive." See "Report Reveals 2.2 Million Borrowers Face Foreclosure on Subprime Home Loans; Homeowners to Lose Billions," Center for Responsible Lending, December 19, 2006, http://www.responsiblelending.org/issues/mortgage/reports/page.jsp?itemID=31214551 (accessed April 12, 2007).

CHAPTER 3
An Examination of a Noble Sentiment

Following Adam Smith, I have argued that items of decency are wholly customary, as determined by a given society. Americans need only consult their guts to ascertain which other types of products are, in the collective American judgment, items of decency: healthcare, yes; cosmetic surgery, no; free, quality education through a child's formative years, yes; Ivy League education from cradle to grave, no; daycare, yes; maid or nanny service, no; home ownership, yes; mansion ownership, no; a reliable vehicle yes; Escalade, Lexus, or even a brand new car, no; access to nutritious foods to prepare at home, yes; resources to dine out frequently, no. This thought experiment can go on and on. If Smith and I are correct, the overwhelming majority of Americans will agree time and again about which types of products are, strictly speaking, luxurious, decent, or necessary.

Not everyone accepts such democratic notions, however. More than one hundred years ago, William Graham Sumner criticized the idea of decent lives as one measure of good nation. Sumner was a social Darwinist, a believer in the doctrine that people's social station in life is largely a function of their genetic "fitness," that the most and least socially fit naturally rise and fall as society evolves, and that government interference in this process of social evolution is not just imprudent, but futile.

In 1887 Sumner published "An Examination of a Noble Sentiment," which challenges the idea "that we ought to see to it that everyone has an existence worthy of a human being." Of this idea—which is strikingly similar to our idea of "decent lives"—Sumner asked five questions, the answers to which appear to transform the foundation of decent lives in national custom into a figment of the economic imagination. Considering Sumner's criticisms will introduce several of the key themes and arguments of subsequent chapters, and this will also help to dispel any doubts about American consensus over items of decency and the indignity connected with their absence.[1]

QUESTION 1: WHAT IS AN EXISTENCE WORTHY OF A HUMAN BEING?

Sumner:

The hod-carrier, who is earning a dollar a day, will say that it is what he could get for a dollar and a half; the mechanic at two dollars will say that it would cost three; a man whose income is a thousand dollars will say that it costs fifteen hundred. I once heard a man, whose salary was twelve thousand dollars, speak of five thousand a year as misery. A [decent life], therefore, at the first touch gives us the first evidence of something wrong. It sounds like a concrete and definite thing, but it is not such; a [decent life] is the most shifting and slippery notion which the human mind can try to conceive. In general it is about fifty percent more than each one of us is getting now, which would, for a time, mean happiness, prosperity, and welfare to us all. It is to be remembered, also, that most of the people who, not in their own opinion, but that of their neighbors, have not a [decent life] are those who do not like that kind of an existence or want it, but have turned their backs upon it, and are in fact rather more contented than any other class of people with their situation as they are now.

The commentary above does not respond to the question, "How much does one need in order to lead a decent life?" but rather responds to the question, "How much does one need in order to be completely happy?" Many would agree that if the question were "How much do you need to be completely happy?" nearly everyone's answer would be "A little more than I have right now." But that is not the question. Answers to the question, "How much does one need to live a decent life?" will be more reserved and focused, for, within a given society, the content of socially decent lives is far less subjective than is the content of individual happiness. While many people would be happier with larger televisions and fancier vehicles, few would have the gall to count these items as customary to decent living in the United States.

"How much does one need in order to lead a decent life?" is also an inadequate question, however, in that it insists that items of decency be defined by assigning a dollar amount. Thinking about the question in terms of number of dollars demands that we estimate the total cost of every item of decency, artificially increasing the likelihood of inconsistent answers. A better question is "What items are essential to a decent life?" In the United States, the answers to this question will prove remarkably clear and consistent: adequate food, shelter, healthcare, insurance, and education are certainly among them. Rewarding work, an owned home, and a reliable vehicle may be included. There will be some disagreement at the margins, but there remains a huge core of consensus. So Sumner is mistaken that the itemized content of decent lives is elusive. Much of it is as clear as day when asked of the people of the same nation.

Sumner then argues that one person's idea of happiness is not universalizable, for other people's ideas of happiness will vary greatly. The monk, the mercenary, and the Mennonite may each be completely happy in virtue of being who they are, but they would be completely unhappy being any one of the others. This is true as to happiness. But all of them equally want the items that comprise the standard for a decent life. Each wants food, shelter, resources to remain healthy, and education to develop his or her talents. Within a given society, the content of a decent life is shared and so, for the most part, is universalizable.

QUESTION 2: FOR HOW MANY PEOPLE MUST A DECENT LIFE BE PROVIDED?

Sumner:

[T]he man who is to be provided with such an existence, under the new arrangement proposed, will not have any such difficulty to contend with; he is to have a living secured to him by the state, or the social reformers, or somebody else. His wife and children will obviously have as good a claim to a [decent life] as he; their support will therefore cause him no anxiety and no burden. Therefore, this class of persons will increase with great rapidity. They are, of course, all those who have neglected or refused to win a [decent life] for themselves; and whenever it is determined that somebody else shall give it to them, it is provided that their number shall multiply indefinitely and forever.

Furthermore, in all these propositions the fact is overlooked that no humanitarian proposition is valid unless it is applied to the whole human race. If I am bound to love my fellow man, it is for reasons which apply to Laplanders and Hottentots just as much as to my neighbor across the street; our obligation to provide a [decent life] is just as great toward Africans or Mongolians as towards Americans. It must certainly be as wide as all human beings. There are millions of people on the globe whose mode of life is far below that of the most miserable wretch in the United States, never has been any better than it is, never will be any better as far ahead as anybody can see, and they cannot be said to be to blame for it. It is true that they do not know that they are badly off; they do not bother their heads about a [decent life.] They do not work much and they are quite free

from care—very much more so than the average American taxpayer.
But, if we are to give a [decent life] to those who have not got it, just
because they have not got it (and no other reason is alleged in connection with the proposition before us), then the persons to whom I
have referred have a very much stronger claim, for they are very
much further away from it.

Sumner raises two challenges here. Both challenges allege the
impracticability and, suggestively, the immorality of providing items
of decency for all. I will call Sumner's first challenge the *problem of
propagation.*

Suppose that all Americans were entitled to items of decency and
that government was required to provide it to those who could not
obtain it for themselves. Unless the government also prohibits individuals dependent upon the state from having children, their children will
also be entitled to government provision of decent lives, and so on.
Sumner suggests that relieving individuals of responsibility for earning
a living will encourage propagation of more dependent offspring.

The rule Sumner relies on is a principle of economics: activity
levels increase when individuals do not have to internalize the costs of
their actions. In a world where government unconditionally guarantees
items of decency for all, more people will have more children than in
a world where everyone has to pay the full costs of childbirth and
rearing. Although many Americans will choose to have few or no children, those Americans whose child-birthing activities increase will
create greater strain upon government resources.

The problem of propagation is one Americans are familiar with.
Many believe that it is at work whenever they see women on welfare
who also have multiple young children. Although I think Sumner is
mistaken on this point, I leave it to the reader to decide whether the
problem of propagation is a strong enough reason to prevent the state
from attempting to guarantee items of decency, for his second challenge is more interesting.

I will call Sumner's second challenge the *problem of humanitari-*

anism. According to Sumner, guaranteeing items of decency for anyone anywhere requires guaranteeing decent lives for everyone everywhere.[2] Sumner's suggestion is that, if taken seriously, humanitarianism transcends nationalism. Those who would devote America's resources toward guaranteeing items of decency for all have no good reason to limit the service to Americans or for even preferring Americans to poor people in other countries.

The argument of *The Unaffordable Nation* is not humanitarian in character. Therefore, I do not share Sumner's concern. But I will say that Sumner and I mean different things by requiring government to guarantee items of decency. Sumner means the actual provision of items of decency to any and all that need them. By contrast, I mean the opportunity of every person to earn items of decency through their labor. The chief obligation of government in the way of ensuring access to items of decency is action to maintain a structure of opportunity within which everyone willing to work hard can earn resources sufficient to afford the basics of a decent life. The problem is not how many of the shiftless will require Medicaid, but how few of the hardworking can afford healthcare.

QUESTION 3: WHAT WILL BE THE EFFECT ON THE PEOPLE OF SECURING THEM A DECENT LIFE?

Sumner:

> Plainly it must be to pauperize them, that is, to take away all hope that they can ever win such an existence for themselves. If not, and if the proposition means only that we hope and strive to make our community as prosperous as possible, and to give everybody in it as good chances as possible, then that is just what we are trying to do

now, to the best of our ability, and the proposal is only an impertinence; it interrupts and disturbs us without contributing anything to
the matter in hand. Now it is one of the worst social errors to pau-
perize people; it demoralizes them through and through; it ruins their
personal character and makes them socially harmful; it lowers their
aims and makes sure that they will never have good ones; it corrupts
their family life and makes sure that they will entail sordid and
unworthy principles of action on their children. If any argument
could be brought forward for an attempt to secure to everyone an
existence worthy of a man, it would be that, in that way, everyone
among us might be worthy to be a human being; but, whenever that
attempt is made, the only result will be that those who get an existence worthy of a human being in that way are sure to be morally
degraded below any admissible standard of human worth.

Here, Sumner reveals himself to be an economic optimist of sorts,
describing the mission of decent lives as an "impertinence," because it
"means only that we hope and strive to make our community as prosperous as possible, and to give everybody in it as good chances as possible," and "that is just what we are trying to do now, to the best of our
ability." This is much like saying that this economic America is perfect insofar as it is the best that anyone could expect in the way of life
chances.

But Sumner also suggests that the mission of decent lives will
actually leave individuals worse off by robbing them of the desire to
become self-sufficient. The lion taken from the wild and fed ready cuts
of antelope will eventually lose some of its will to hunt. But it will take
a lot of free antelope. Likewise, the lion born in captivity will never
entirely lose the will to hunt no matter how much free antelope you
feed it. That is why no one is willing to walk through their cages. If
Sumner is to be believed, however, to lend the less-well-off a helping
hand is simultaneously to destroy within them every iota of the desire
for self-sufficiency. To even permit an American to taste government
support, or the support of his fellow man, is for Sumner the equivalent
of the crack addict's first and purest high.

Sumner's answer to question 3 (and question 4 below) is representative of a bias that is common among Americans even a century later: that to help another person via the provision of resources is simultaneously to harm them horribly. This theme is so central to Americans' thinking about economic responsibility that it is the subject of the next chapter. For now, it suffices to observe that while the desire for self-sufficiency can be affected by the provision of welfare aid, the threat does not rise to the cataclysmic level that Sumner supposes. Nor, I shall argue, is the risk of dependency on social aid a strong enough reason to withhold it from those who need it and those who are willing to work.

QUESTION 4: WHO IS TO SECURE DECENT LIVES FOR THE AFORESAID PERSONS?

Sumner:

> Evidently it can only be those who have already, no one knows by which struggles and self-denial, won it for themselves. This proposition, like all the others of the class to which it belongs, proposes to smite with new responsibilities, instead of rewards, the man who has done whatever everyone ought to do. We are told what fine things would happen if every one of us would go and do something for the welfare of somebody else; but why not contemplate also the immense gain which would ensue if everybody would do something for himself? The latter is ever so much more reasonable than the former; for those who are now taking care of themselves have very little strength to spare, while those who are not now taking care of themselves might do a great deal more. The plan of securing to those who have not a [decent life] that blessing, is a plan for leaving the latter at ease and putting more load on the former; to the society, therefore, it is doubly destructive, increasing its burdens and wasting its resources at the same time.

I appreciate Sumner's observation that there are many Americans who could do more to provide for themselves than they are currently doing. The argument of part 2 is that there are important differences between Americans who are doing their best but failing, and Americans who are failing, in part, because they are not doing their best. Although the two are difficult to distinguish in practice, Americans are truly only against the latter group.

I also agree with Sumner that any nation is better off when the hardworking do not have to work incrementally harder to support those who are failing. Here is the ill-fated fact about economically dysfunctional people, however. They will cost us no matter what we do. Investment may coax some to live full, productive lives, or at least to limit counterproductivity. Alternatively, there are the costs of noninvestment: greater crime, poorer health, less education, scourge. We will pay either way: education or law enforcement; health preservation or treatment of greater, more extensive illnesses; drug addiction or drug prescription. The only decision that is ours is how we prefer to pay.

QUESTION 5: WHAT MEANS ARE TO BE USED TO GIVE A DECENT LIFE TO EVERYBODY?

Sumner:

> To this, there is no answer; we are left to conjecture. The most reasonable conjecture is that the proponents themselves do not know; they have not made up their minds; they have not really faced the question. A proposition to give everybody an existence worthy of a human being, without a specification of the measures by which it is proposed to do it, is like a proposition to make everybody handsome.

The humanitarian impulse is often blind. It passionately insists that all human suffering has a cure but is mute when pressed for what any cure is. Many Americans hold this kind of naive humanitarianism, unable to accept that they shall never be able to entirely purge their fair land of suffering. Even so, Sumner misses how fundamental the ability to afford items of decency through labor is to the American conception of economic justice. For the most part, that belief *is* the American conception of economic justice. Such justice is not about receiving assistance from the government but is about earning through one's own industry.

Protecting against unaffordability with labor, then, is a fundamental purpose for which the United States exists, and the absence of such protections signals a fundamental shift in the whole project of the American nation.

NOTES

1. What I refer to as *decent lives* Sumner names with the German *menschenwürdiges Dasein*. For my purposes, there is no concern over what is lost in translation. These excerpts are taken from Jerry Muller, ed., *Conservatism: An Anthology of Social and Political Thought from David Hume to the Present* (Princeton, NJ: Princeton University Press, 1997), pp. 245–48.

2. The problem of humanitarianism is well illustrated by religious prayer. To the honest person, it never feels quite right to say a prayer for only a subset of humanity, whether it be a single relative, your favorite sports team, the Religious Right, the Church of England, or the peoples of Mozambique. The humanitarian impulse behind prayer constantly pushes the penitent man to expand the scope of his prayer to all of humanity. However, at that point, the potency of the prayer feels so diluted as to make impossible the result for which he descended to his knees.

CHAPTER 4
The Billionaire and the Destitute Man: Unaffordability as a Political Problem

As to the experience of unaffordability with labor, America's leading political parties offer very different narrative explanations: these are social injustice and personal irresponsibility.

Using the narrative of social injustice, the Democratic platform contends that greater regulation and redistribution of wealth are needed to improve the economic lives of the middle and lower classes, who, despite a political system that subjugates its own legitimate interests to wealthier illegitimate ones, might succeed by their own industry. Due to the real or perceived characters of their constituency, the Democratic platform tends to view "isms"—racism, sexism, homophobism, classism—as the primary causes of unaffordability with labor. Conversely, the platform treads lightly, if not altogether avoids, plausible explanations of unaffordability with labor grounded in constituent members' personal failings. As consequence, the Democratic platform is regularly at a loss for words when forced to condemn poor choosers, who happen also to be traditional or other social minorities.

Using the narrative of personal irresponsibility, the Republican platform contends that, far from greater government regulation, what the industrious (meaning themselves) need is far less government intervention, which will result in increased personal resources across

the board and, with it, spurred economic activity. The Republican platform makes little mention of the social inequalities that continue to
skew many Americans' life chances or that cut those chances short for
persons before reaching adulthood. Through repeated lobbies to
reduce taxes for America's top individual and corporate earners, and
resistance to egalitarian reforms in such basic areas as education and
healthcare, the Republican platform effectively signals to its base its
default position that unaffordability with labor is an illusion; that, in
fact, all unaffordability in America is due to individual irresponsibility,
a predicament wholly undeserving of governmental response.

Whatever truth there may be in the party narratives of social justice and individual responsibility for contemporary Americans, they
are equally inadequate as explanations for the unaffordable nation. It
is neither social justice nor individual irresponsibility that accounts
for the fact that today many laboring Americans struggle to earn
items of decency. Institutional discrimination is indispensable to
understanding why certain social groupings in the United States are
disproportionately poor and dramatically underrepresented in the
upper classes in terms of education, prestige, salary, and wealth. But
institutional discrimination cannot explain why so many Americans
with full-time jobs, of every race, gender, and, sexual orientation, find
it difficult to afford the full complement of items of decency. Likewise, for the most part, the explanation of individual irresponsibility
simply does not apply to Americans who consistently work full-time
jobs.

Thus, while social justice and personal responsibility have their
place in the moral calculus of the unaffordable nation (see part 2) and
help account for the facts of unaffordability for some, the concern here
is the generic reality of unaffordability with labor, which requires a
different accounting.

An exchange at the close of the 109th Congress provides an
important clue. To repeat an earlier point, the federal minimum wage
has languished at $5.15 per hour since 1997. To my knowledge, no
person in either political party alleges that $5.15 per hour is a reason-

able or fair wage for contemporary America, or one that any person in the United States could live decently on. In the same nine-year period since Congress last voted to increase the minimum wage, Congress has routinely voted to grant itself raises, by most estimates in excess of $30,000, though this fact is of limited anecdotal value.

On August 18, 2005, Representative George Miller (D-CA) introduced House Resolution 2429, the Fair Minimum Wage Act of 2005, which proposed to increase the federal minimum wage to $5.85 per hour sixty days following passage of the resolution, $6.55 one year hence, and $7.25 two years hence. Other versions of the act were proposed, such as Senator Hillary Clinton's (D-NY) Standing with Minimum Wage Earners Act of 2006, but with essentially the same increases in minimum wage and time lines.[1]

The version of the Fair Minimum Wage Act of 2005 ultimately placed on the Senate calendar for approval had attached to it—and therefore became conditioned upon passage of—House Resolution 5970, the Estate Tax and Extension of Tax Relief Act of 2006. Introduced by Representative William Thomas (R-CA) on July 28, 2006, this act would have amended the Internal Revenue Code to increase the unified tax credit against estate taxes (the so-called "death tax") according to the following schedule: 2010—$3,750,000; 2011—$4,000,000; 2012—$4,250,000; 2013—$4,500,000; 2014—$4,750,000; 2015 and thereafter— $5,000,000. The credit would be made available to individuals and their spouses, for a credit against estate taxes in the event of death in the amount of $10,000,000 per household.

The political result was that in order for Congress to raise the federal minimum wage to $7.25 for the poorest American workers following a ten-year wage stagnation, Congress would have to grant the richest Americans $10 million of insulation against taxes upon their accumulated wealth. The bill failed in the Senate by a vote of 56–42 on August 4, 2006. On the heels of another largely failed Congress, Democrats blamed Republicans for their willingness to sacrifice the working poor to serve millionaires and billionaires, and Republicans blamed Democrats for their unwillingness to recognize the destructive consequences of requiring the wealthiest Americans to pay taxes on their estates upon death.

There were slim concessions to be made on either side: only 3 percent of Americans actually were earning the minimum wage of $5.15, but millions more were earning so little from their full-time work that they were unable to afford items of decency. Also, in limited cases, estate taxes can result in substantial disadvantages to closely held businesses, although the benefit accrues mainly to wealthy Americans who can scarcely imagine insolvency for themselves or their businesses.

The finger-pointing over yet another failure by the American Congress to increase the minimum wage obscured the larger moral significance of this legislative imbroglio. The failure illustrates the inability of Americans, through their political representatives, to fairly weigh and prioritize the interests of justice. Supposing the current estate tax regime is, in fact, an unfair tax burden on the wealthiest Americans, there remains the question of whether the interests of millionaires and billionaires in repealing estate taxes equals or outweighs the interests of low-income Americans in being able to afford items of decency by their labor. There is also the question of whether the interests of millionaires and billionaires in abolishing estate taxes justified the radical step of withholding from the working disadvantaged economic relief that everyone agrees is necessary and clearly overdue, unless and until controversial estate tax reforms occur.

Some justice concerns cannot be played against each other, making it both despicable and unfair to attempt to compare or barter them for political purposes. For example, it would be morally indefensible to accept Abraham Lincoln's Emancipation Proclamation freeing all slaves only if certain international tariffs were relaxed or taxes were abolished on certain products moving through interstate commerce. Likewise, holding up efforts to make life affordable for all working Americans until the richest Americans obtain special tax breaks is reprehensible, even if there are good arguments that estate taxes themselves are unduly burdensome.

Note that there have been many other legislative failures to increase the federal minimum wage, including the Fair Minimum Wage Act of 2004, the Fair Minimum Wage Act of 2003, the Fair Minimum Wage Act of 2002, the Fair Minimum Wage Act of 2001, the Fair Minimum Wage Act of 2000, the Fair Minimum Wage Act of 1999, and so on.[2] Attempts to pass a Fair Minimum Wage Act in 2007 were under way, after control of the House and the Senate fell to the Democrats in the November 2006 congressional elections, but the issues that prevented passage of all of the prior acts remain.

Congress's inability to increase the federal minimum wage despite apparent consensus between Republicans and Democrats that such an increase is mandated by fairness raises *politics* as an alternative explanation of unaffordability with labor. Not "politics" in the ordinary, 103rd through 109th congressional failure to increase the minimum wage sense of that term, but rather "politics" in the broader, cultural sense of how Americans seek to balance capitalism and democracy.

Many scholars have observed that advanced capitalism and advanced democracy face incompatibilities. In their infancies, capitalism and democracy are mutually reinforcing, even needful of each another. Ousting kings and toppling oligarchs go hand in hand with free trade and fair taxation. The two are born of and thrive within the same soil. But gods who play together as children compete and fight as adults. In their later stages of maturation, the full identities of the two regulatory systems begin to manifest and the continued advancement of one comes to depend on subjugation of the other.

As an ideal, the perfection of democracy requires that every citizen enjoy a threshold level of material equality, which can be maintained only through mindful regulation and redistribution of capital. Again, as an ideal, the perfection of capitalism requires regulation that enhances the ease and the security of market transactions, such as a strong central banking system that is our Federal Reserve. The same ideal of capitalist perfection prohibits the distribution of capital according to *who* people are, even on such noble bases as citizenship or residency. Instead, the ideal demands that capital be distributed exclusively according to the value of what people do as judged by other people.

The tensions between advanced capitalism and advanced democracy are manifest in the lives of everyday citizens. People for whom capitalism is the predominant value experience not the slightest twinge of conscience at observing a destitute man alongside a billionaire. These facts, in themselves, are morally insignificant. What matters to such people is that neither the destitute man nor the billionaire has reached their stations in life through trampling upon the economic rights of others. Even if the billionaire is a product of inheritance and the destitute man the product of a broken home, economic justice obtains so long as the billionaire has respected the property rights of others and the destitute man has not had any of his property rights violated.

At most, such persons pity the destitute man, and perhaps they make a charitable contribution. They will not suspect that injustice is afoot. The faith of people for whom capitalism is the predominant value is that any person can succeed by personal effort. This predisposes them to believe that the lot of the destitute man has been decided by his own misjudgments. Ruling that out, such people will look for acts of God that, while possibly unjust in a divine sense, do not warrant reordering economic entitlements. Perhaps the destitute man is from a dysfunctional family or was born with birth defects. A primordial shame but not a political crime!

The sight of a billionaire alongside a destitute man is a matter of grave and immediate concern to those for whom democracy is the predominant value. These people are convinced that a fundamental connection exists between material well-being and the capacity for meaningful political participation. Typically, such people are attuned to the fact that politics is susceptible to manipulation by those who hold great concentrations of wealth, making suffrage and advancement of personal causes far more accessible to billionaires than to destitute men. Such people also believe that the range of natural talents and nurtured abilities is not so great across humanity as to fully account for the existence of billionaires and destitute men within the same society.

Those who believe democracy is the predominant value are not inherently averse to great disparities in wealth. People who insist that the existence within the same society of billionaires and destitute men is inherently unjust are motivated by socialistic rather than democratic concern. Americans who believe that democracy is suffering because of capitalism want to control the flow of wealth only to the extent necessary to neutralize the political inequality it produces. Such persons are often suspected of socialist sympathies because their measures could conceivably also serve that end. However, that is not why they support them.

The ideals of capitalism and democracy just explained compete within the mind of every American. Which ideal wins out is often fleeting and contextual. The capitalist identity surfaces most strongly when confronted with lazy or incompetent workers and other individuals who, in one's estimation, refuse to accept full responsibility for their lives. The democratic identity controls when genuine cases of the inability to afford items of decency are observed in spite of hard work and when rich and powerful citizens are exposed for having criminally used government for their own ends. Hybrid feelings emerge when observing the poor and homeless on the streets. Alongside compassion is a question whether the paths of such people are paved mainly by poor luck, poor choice, or poor justice. We would treat them differently depending on the truth of the matter.

Consider now how differently proposals to increase the federal minimum wage are likely interpreted by Americans who view the world primarily through capitalist or democratic lenses. Through their political representatives, people for whom capitalism is the predominant value will support political agendas meant to shore up economic freedom, whether by reducing individual or corporate taxation, privatization of social services, piecemeal eradication of welfare programs, and so on. These people may have no special objections to increasing the federal minimum wage, but the proposal itself symbolizes a larger set of political commitments to which, at the moment, they principally object. Through their political representatives, people for whom democracy is the predominant value will support political agendas meant to shore up basic welfare through graduated taxation and regulation of basic goods, services, and the private entities that would otherwise dominate them. For these people, increasing the federal minimum wage could not be more important, for the passage of this type of legislation is for them a bellwether of good nation.

The casualties of this difference in political vision are those who continue to receive disgracefully inadequate wages for their labor. In this way, the origins of unaffordability with labor may be located in American culture rather than in any fundamental economic policy, and the failures of the 103rd through 109th Congresses to increase the federal minimum wage are merely the result.[3]

To this point, readers may have been under the impression that the unaffordable nation is a phenomenon that *happens to* nations rather than a state of affairs *chosen or acquiesced into* by them. Free markets have and will always produce periods of economic hardship, periods in which not all members of a society are able to afford items of decency. The perpetual question is how, if at all, a nation responds. It is good government that sees nations through such times, via recognition that during these times only regulatory action can preserve economic affordability. The unaffordable nation arises when capitalism produces hardships that reduce economic affordability below the level needed for laboring members of a society to afford items of decency, and government either refuses to take or is incapable of taking action.

Persons laboring in an unaffordable nation can still procure items of decency by doing more than they reasonably should have to in the way of work, perhaps even achieving an enviable quality of life. The unaffordable nation is not measured by rates of economic desolation but is measured by the level of well-being that the American people believe all hardworking members should enjoy for the amounts of labor that the same people identify as reasonable. Thus, it is no retort to the unaffordable nation that the average incomes of Americans have raised or that few Americans live in abject poverty. The issue is that even with such incomes and the nonexistence of absolute poverty, many hard-working Americans cannot afford the items of decency that they believe should be accessible for everyone who is working full-time.

It is a common, everyday occurrence when members of Congress and our president publicly remark upon how difficult it has become for the average American family to afford items of decency. What they do not say, and what I have tried to show, is that the uncooperative state of our legislature, along with ideological stubbornness of our executive branch, is not the primary cause of unaffordability with labor in America. Rather, the ultimate source of the disagreements reflected in government is traceable to the American people themselves.

In a way, this conclusion should be obvious. Americans should expect their own political disagreements to find expression in the activity and votes of their political representatives. But I want to suggest that there is something special about American disagreement over such issues as simple and straightforward as increasing the federal minimum wage. Often, the way Americans speak about government and the citizenry reveals an assumption that we truly are one people. That is, Americans of all political stripes appear to continue to believe that any of our political disagreements are overshadowed by, and minuscule as compared to, the fundamental tenets of American freedom shared by all Americans.

There have been enough Americans to block, through their political representatives, an increase in the federal minimum wage for more than a decade running. Meanwhile, no American is willing to defend the view that $5.15 per hour is enough to build a decent life through labor. Either many Americans no longer believe that every person should be able to afford a decent life through their labor, or they are simply proceeding in bad faith—refusing to support reforms that they acknowledge are required by justice because they have self-interested reasons for not wanting justice to occur.

In that case, there is no point complaining any longer to our political representatives to act. Rather, it is time to revisit the tenets of American freedom themselves and to figure out whether or not they truly are still American values. The idea that every American ought to be able to earn a decent life by his or her own labor is not an American value if only the poor and powerless endorse it. Indeed, the poor and the powerless of virtually every nation probably believe the same thing.

Rather, in order for the idea of decent lives in exchange for full-time work to be an *American* value, it must be held by rich and poor alike. Again, in order for that idea to be an *American* value, Americans with the power to influence change must be just as outraged by the inability of many full-time workers to earn decent lives as the workers failing by their labor themselves. The record of the 103rd through 109th Congresses suggests that this is not the case; our Congresses have merely been paying lip service to an idea that might have been an American value sometime in the nation's past, but it is really no longer a priority.

So, the unaffordable nation is a political problem, manifested in the gridlocked American government but rooted fundamentally in an American economic culture that apparently is in transition. By and large, Americans have reacted to these cultural growing pains dismissively, if not childishly, assuming that anyone who disagrees with them must be acting in bad faith and taking their own beliefs to represent the whole and obvious truth.

America's political parties only add fuel to this misconduct. Through party rhetoric, each pretends that the restoration of economic affordability turns mainly on whether Americans vote Democrat or Republican, and whether they lean liberally or conservatively. This approach to addressing the unaffordable nation carries heavy social costs. For one, character assassination among the political parties— Democrats say "Republicans," Republicans say "Democrats," liberals say "conservatives," conservatives say "liberals"—has reduced these political designations to little more than political slurs.

In the current political climate, the designations are more often used as an *ad hominem* attack to tarnish another's reputation instead of to identify oneself with a unique set of political values. As commonly employed, the designations are the equivalent of saying "political nigger" or "political bitch"—nothing more. Ready reliance on these political stereotypes also leaves many citizens less capable of defending, or even of coherently explaining, their own political values.

If the intractability of the unaffordable nation is an issue of political culture rather than ordinary politics, then the proper focus of discussion is on the political culture from which these divisive beliefs arise. The remainder of the book argues that a unique economic morality persists in the United States, an economic morality that assigns special significance to individual labor and that contemplates certain social entitlements grounded in hard work. That economic morality inhabits the American moral conscience in the form of a social contract setting forth in broad outline private and public responsibilities regarding workers, here understood as a regulated social institution integral to the continued existence and flourishing of the United States.

The American economic morality may serve as a relatively independent standard for measuring common political attitudes regarding the unaffordable nation. Parts 2 and 3 reconstruct each side of this social contract. Part 2 deals with the individual responsibility of Americans to meet certain thresholds of labor and to work well, and part 3 deals with the social guarantees and other protections that American government is obligated to extend to working Americans for having done so.

NOTES

1. Interestingly, Senator Hillary Clinton's version of the bill would have automatically increased the minimum wage in any given year by the same percentage "by which the annual rate of pay for Members of Congress increased for such year."

2. On this issue, see Jerold Waltman, *The Politics of the Minimum Wage* (Champaign: University of Illinois Press, 2000).

3. On May 24, 2007, shortly before this book went to press, Congress approved an increase in the minimum wage from $5.15 to $7.25 over two years. As the increase was part of a larger spending package that includes nearly $100 billion in funds for military operations in Iraq and Afghanistan, President Bush was likely to sign the bill.

PART 2:
POOR CHOICE, POOR JUSTICE, POOR LUCK

Introduction:
Labor Obligations and Excuses

D o Americans have an obligation to work? If so, what is the nature of that social obligation? How much, in what ways, when, and for whom? What is the price of not working? And what should happen where honest labor fails to yield items of decency?

As one side of the social contract that comprises the American economic morality, part 2 examines the moral values underpinning labor expectations in America. Joined together, these values give rise to a culture of individual economic responsibility regulated by an extremely conservative Golden Rule of Labor. A labor-reinforcing feature of this culture of economic responsibility is Americans' belief that the scope of determinism is exceptionally narrow; that is, nearly all of what occurs in the world is traceable to free choices. General faith in radical autonomy supports a presumption that any person in difficult financial circumstances suffers from his or her own avoidable ineptness or bad decision making, which shores up policies against granting exceptions to labor norms.

The principal effect of the Golden Rule of Labor is to place *outside* of the morality of labor virtually all social concerns that do not directly impact the ability to work, including most justice and equity concerns. There are many disciplinary paths from which to approach the American morality of labor as a cultural phenomenon. The most revealing approach for my purposes, however, is through contemplation of the Golden Rule as it informs and circumscribes public policy and through regulating the kinds of legitimate excuses for nonlabor that are made available to individual Americans.

As the framework for the rest of part 2, chapter 5 attempts to describe the American culture of responsibility through a case study— the American hatred of paupers. The dictionary definition of a pauper is "a person without any means of support," but more especially, "a destitute person who depends upon aid from public welfare funds or charity."[1] Far more than simply a person on the public dole, the pauper is metaphysically a key figure in the politics of every nation. When called upon to explain the reality of pauperism, nations must draw upon their entire repository of cultural knowledge regarding human freedom. Can our paupers be said to have "chosen" their condition? When, if ever, can one's environment be described as stifling or overwhelming free choice? May it matter that some paupers are born of degraded or frail constitution?

Such crucial metaphysical decisions cannot be long postponed in a political society. Quietly, these founding cultural decisions determine whether and to what extent poor choice will factor into a nation's labor expectations, including the circumstances under which nations will provide their paupers social welfare.

The introduction to part 1 explained that fundamentally there are three broad kinds of moral reason for the inability to obtain items of decency through one's labor. These are *poor choice*, *poor justice*, and *poor luck*. These reasons double as possible causal explanations of the condition of pauperism, as well as other economic hardships, including unaffordability with labor. Poor choice is unique and analytically prior to either poor justice or poor luck, however, in that the whole cultural meaning of free choice is bound up with how nations resolve to deal with the reality of pauperism. Put otherwise, only after resolving the cultural meaning of free choice does it become possible to define the social parameters of poor luck and poor justice.

To uncover the American position on poor choice, chapter 5 examines the moral status of two kinds of pauper in the American imagination: the *voluntary* pauper, who has failed to do everything within his or her power to avoid the economic condition, and the *involuntary* pauper, who has done everything within his or her power to avoid the condition but has failed. The examination reveals in the United States a deep moral disgust for voluntary paupers; so deep, in fact, the public policy aspiration is to categorically deny them any social assistance.

An important implication of the American prohibition on assisting voluntary paupers is that, as a matter of public policy, the United States could not be committed to the total eradication of all poverty and other social ills within its borders, for that would mean subsidizing voluntary paupers. This cultural prohibition is also constitutive of the fundamental moral principle issuing in the Golden Rule of Labor: *that every person do his or her absolute, economic best* or risk national abandonment in terms of eligibility for social welfare. On the other hand, the American culture of responsibility supports government assistance to involuntary paupers, such as poor-justice and poor-luck cases, provided that the aid does not improperly relieve individuals of labor obligations that they are capable of carrying.

According to the logic of the American culture of responsibility, under ideal circumstances social welfare would have a major and minor function. In its minor function, social welfare would exist as a floating resource capable of identifying individuals just at the point where they have achieved a socially predetermined threshold of labor, which also proves insufficient for affording items of decency. In that case, social welfare would deposit the difference in resources between what the laborer has been capable of earning and the amount needed to actually purchase the full complement of items of decency.

In its major function, social welfare would contain a skills-building element designed to wean individuals from the need for the social welfare's minor functions by increasing the market value of the individual's labor. Neither the minor nor major services of social welfare would be made available to persons until they have done all that they reasonably could to provide for themselves. On this reasoning, working well, or at least working satisfactorily, is a primary moral condition of social welfare eligibility. To this end, also, political dissatisfaction with social welfare programs in the United States has little to do with the fact that the United States provides social welfare and has everything to do with the characters of Americans who are either eligible or who actually receive aid.

In any case, by condemning the voluntary pauper, the American culture of responsibility rejects poor choice as a valid excuse for modifying labor obligations, either in the form of reduced amounts of work or unconditional public subsidies. This leaves poor justice and poor luck as possible excuses for relaxing the Golden Rule, here interpreted as legal injustice and social inequity.

With regard to legal injustice, chapter 6 argues that under the American morality of labor, the only injustices that warrant reductions in labor expectations are injustices that have labor-disabling consequences. The inflexibility of the Golden Rule on the subject of legal injustice is illustrated by the rule's refusal even to grant exceptions in cases of discrimination based on immutable characteristics such as race and gender, and also in the rule's attempt to place conditions upon programs of affirmative action that are designed to remedy the continuing effects of discrimination. The concern that aid will undercut the duty to work is the same in the context of affirmative action programs as in the context of social welfare programs, for special opportunities for advancement can ease the labor obligations persons might otherwise carry just as the direct delivery of economic resources can.

With regard to social inequity, chapter 7 considers the impact upon the Golden Rule of labor-affecting mental or physical disabilities and of economic limitations resulting from inadequate structural opportunities. Here, the conclusions are much less tidy than for poor choice or poor justice, because disabled persons often receive treatment inconsistent with the Golden Rule. Also, after a certain point the lack of structural opportunities is more aptly described as social injustice rather than mere social inequity. Despite these complexities, even in the case of social inequity, the Golden Rule remains resolute and unforgiving and gives way only in the most extreme of cases.

The end result of the American morality of labor and its enforcer, the Golden Rule, is unsurprising and somewhat depressing: the individual obligation not just to work but to always satisfy the nation's labor expectations is an inescapable demand. Any who run afoul of this morality of labor are met with heavy ostracism, not unlike expatriates in residence.

NOTE

1. http://dictionary.reference.com/browse/pauper (accessed September 20, 2006).

CHAPTER 5
Poor Choice: The American Hatred of Paupers

The native American poor never lose their delicacy or pride; hence, though unreduced to the physical degradation of the European pauper, they yet suffer more in mind than the poor of any other people in the world. Those peculiar social sensibilities nourished by our own peculiar political principles, while they enhance the true dignity of the prosperous American, do but minister to the added wretchedness of the unfortunate; first, by prohibiting their acceptance of what little random relief charity may offer; and, second, by furnishing them with the keenest appreciation of the smarting distinction between their ideal of universal equality and their grindstone experience of the practical misery and infamy of poverty—a misery and infamy which is, ever has been, and ever will be, precisely the same in India, England, and America.

—Herman Melville, *Poor Man's Pudding*

There is no possible definition of "a poor man." A pauper is a person who cannot earn his living; whose producing powers have fallen positively below his necessary consumption; who cannot, therefore, pay his way. A human society needs the active co-operation and productive energy of every person in it. A man who is present as a consumer, yet who does not contribute either by land, labor, or capital to the work of society, is a burden. On no sound political theory ought such a person to share in the political power of the State. He drops out of the ranks of workers and producers. Society must support him. It accepts the burden, but he must be cancelled from the ranks of the rulers likewise. So much for the pauper. About him no more need be

103

said. But he is not the "poor man." The "poor man" is an elastic term, under which any number of social fallacies may be hidden. . . . Under the [name] of the poor . . . the negligent, shiftless, inefficient, silly, and imprudent are fastened upon the industrious and prudent as a responsibility and a duty. On the one side, the terms are extended to cover the idle, intemperate, and vicious, who, by the combination, gain credit which they do not deserve, and which they could not get if they stood alone. On the other hand, the terms are extended to include wage-receivers of the humblest rank, who are degraded by the combination. The reader who desires to guard himself against fallacies should always scrutinize the [term] "poor" as used, so as to · see which or how many of these classes they are made to cover.

—William Graham Sumner,
What Social Classes Owe to Each Other

s evidenced by Melville and Sumner above, the pauper is a unique creature in the American moral imagination. First, the pauper is commonly believed capable of doing more than he currently is doing in the promotion of his own well-being. To the extent that the pauper realizes his own power but neglects it, and instead seeks satisfaction through dependence upon others, his pauperism is *voluntary*. Second, the pauper who grows accustomed to economic dependence may not just neglect his own power but may lose sight of its very existence; that is, he may come to believe that his sole means of getting along is through charity. To the extent the pauper is convinced that his station is beyond his control, although false, his pauperism is *involuntary*, not in the popular sense of lacking willfulness or physical control, but in one legal sense of being not fully intentional or premeditated (but see the discussion of Kant and the vices below). Whereas the involuntary pauper is a moral tragedy, the voluntary pauper is a moral anathema.

As I have defined the terms, both voluntary and involuntary paupers are equivalent to Sumner's "poor men"—economically negligent, shiftless, inefficient, silly, imprudent, idle, intemperate, and vicious men. I believe the terms voluntary and involuntary paupers are better (and certainly less pejorative) descriptions of such persons, if only because the distinction accounts for nuanced psychological varieties of experience at play with persons dependent on public assistance. Also, as I use the term, "poor" refers to certain levels of economic deprivation rather than to any underlying causes of the same. On this usage, the class "the [economic] poor" is morally divisible into voluntary and involuntary paupers, but also *non-voluntary* paupers, people who suffer economic deprivation due to unaffordability with labor that meets established labor expectations.

Earlier, in considering "the effect on the people of securing them a decent life," Sumner claimed that the inevitable result was pauperism, "that is, to take away all hope that they can ever win such an existence for themselves." Recall that I have a different view of the government's primary role in ensuring the availability of items of decency. But if it were true that the primary cause of pauperism in America was social welfare, Americans would rightly not support it. But is it true? Have we a reliable standard to judge?

The American culture of responsibility comprises one such standard of evaluation, according to which the facilitation of pauperism is a clear risk of social welfare, but social welfare is not an independent cause of pauperism. For Americans, moreover, the risks of promoting pauperism do not outweigh the benefits of maintaining a welfare state, and it is believed these risks are capable of being minimized by properly safeguarding the programs.

THE AMERICAN CULTURE OF RESPONSIBILITY

The project of administering rules of responsibility is the same in all nations that have embraced the reality of human freedom. The first order of business is never to impose responsibility where freedom is lacking. The second order of business is to always impose responsibility where freedom is present. Free nations are identical in this respect. However, our imperfect natures make the administration of responsibility likewise imperfect, mandating choices about whether it is best to err on the side of too much or too little responsibility enforcement.

No matter what rules of responsibility a nation adopts, they will inevitably sweep too broadly at times—imposing responsibility for states of affair beyond the control of persons—and sweep too narrowly at other times—withholding responsibility for states of affair within the control of persons. For example, historical assumptions about the inability of women to control their emotions contributed to their legally mandated relief from participating in politics and the workplace, denying them the ability both to earn a living for themselves and to equally advocate for their political beliefs. This is an example of attributing too little responsibility to a particular group. As another example, for much of America's history, genuine mental disability was not, or was only inadequately, recognized as an excuse from liability for conduct that would otherwise constitute crimes under the law. This is an example of attributing too much responsibility to a particular group. Nations correct these errors only as they become convinced of their mistakes, and will inevitably commit more mistakes than they ever catch.

Any nation will deal with both situations many times throughout its history. Through the rules of responsibility it settles upon, however, each nation ensures that much more of one and much less of the other kind of error comes to pass. Each nation must choose for itself which kind of error is the more palatable one, the least offensive to its sense of economic justice. As a result, some nations are quite lax about economic responsibility, making state aid available independent of economic hardship or of whether one has made a good-faith effort at self-sufficiency. Meanwhile, other nations view economic responsibility as among their highest priorities, placing substantial social and moral taxes upon the receipt of state aid.

I submit that the United States is distinctive in its desire to enforce economic responsibility at virtually all costs. Earlier chapters offered some explanation for the rigid American stance on economic responsibility. The core of the American self-conception is that Americans are freestanding individuals, able to make their own ways against all odds. According to that view, individuals unable to advance this ideal are by definition less American: insufficiently industrious, prideful, committed, or capable of the American program of freedom. The United States has bred a people quite comfortable with imposing far greater economic responsibility upon individuals than could be within their scope, because the alternative is too distressing.

Nations also part ways over the ease with which individuals should be spared the consequences of their economic choices. The unflinching enforcement of the harshest rule of economic responsibility may be quite attractive where complemented by a generous policy for helping citizens who have made poor choices. Similarly, the lukewarm enforcement of a moderate rule of economic responsibility may seem tyrannical when accompanied by an unforgiving attitude toward people who have made poor choices. As others have observed, the former kind of regime assigns heavy social stigma to the act of requesting aid, because, in this view, it is necessary to motivate individuals to act responsibly. In nations with harsh rules of responsibility but generous policies for aid, social stigma is the price of the help. Conversely, the latter kind of regime enforces economic responsibility by allowing poor choosers to suffer the greater brunt of their economic mistakes. Such regimes will not judge broken men as harshly but will readily permit them to starve.

Again, I submit there is no question that the United States is the kind of regime that attaches social stigma of aid to promote economic responsibility. If the motto for the other kind of regime is that "it is better not to give," the motto of the United States is that "to give and resent is better than not to have given at all." The resulting culture of responsibility is one in which the request for governmental aid is a serious public act inviting the full scrutiny of the society. Americans understand that they must pay a price—in social respect—for needing public assistance.

At first glance, the idea that a people could prefer a system of economic responsibility that stigmatizes the need for help seems incredible and cruel. People regularly require economic assistance not through any fault of their own but due mainly to poor luck or poor justice. Americans understand this as well as any other people. The preference for taxing the request for assistance is, for Americans, the lesser of two evils. They would rather stigmatize requests for assistance than force citizens absolutely to live or die by their economic choices. Their public gripes notwithstanding, Americans prefer the welfare state to what they perceive as a more hardhearted alternative.

The lesser of two evils remains an evil, however. That is why the welfare state must always taste bittersweet to Americans. Its very existence disrupts Americans' self-conception as a confederation of individual islands, each preferring but not requiring the collaborative proximity of every other. At the end of the day, Americans lack the courage to erect the society that most accords with their self-ideal. They do not want a nation in which any Atlas is capable of shrugging off the whole world.[1] Such a world is as frightening to Americans as it is romantic.

The begrudging American welfare state represents a deliberate compromise on conflicting but equally important values. Americans seek a system of economic responsibility that exalts the libertarian ideal of man but also a system of economic justice that escapes the certain barbarism of the libertarian society. Viewed from the other direction, Americans seek a socially liberal system of economic justice that reflects their beliefs in communal economic obligation, but they also seek a system of economic responsibility that separates the good will of communitarianism from the perception of entitlement that liberal societies tend to cultivate.

◈

Finally, all nations require a method or set of rules to determine when individuals are entitled to reductions in economic responsibility. The cases that direct Americans' thinking about reductions in economic responsibility are three: children, the disabled, and the elderly. A common denominator among children, some disabled, and some elderly is *incapacity*, regarded as the lack of cognitive or physical ability deemed necessary to carry out all of the duties believed to be part of the economic adulthood.

By extension, Americans who do not fit one of these categories but who still seek reductions in economic obligation must prove that they are similarly situated. Not just any incapacity will serve. Rather, the paradigm cases result in a deliberately narrow definition of incapacity. Because few working-age adult Americans suffer such diagnosed medical or developmental limitations, virtually all Americans are excluded from the definition, making them fully economically able. The hindrances associated with poor upbringing, low intelligence, less-than-adequate work opportunities, and so on, count for little.

A question: if only persons with work-affecting physical or cognitive disabilities are genuinely "incapable" of carrying full economic responsibility, why are so many others—mainly individuals of social disadvantage—the beneficiaries of existing social welfare programs?

First, many welfare beneficiaries are children, themselves incapable, and eligible by virtue of parents who for a wealth of reasons cannot support them. As incapables, children's rights to the benefits of the welfare system should not be conditioned upon the economic character of their chaperones. Second, the class of people who are welfare-eligible in America is broader than the class of people who are technically welfare-deserving. That is so because no social program can be perfectly targeted but also because states lack the wherewithal to aggressively police the boundaries of the welfare-deserving, relying instead upon thresholds. Third, Americans may quietly give credence to the view that physical and cognitive disabilities are not the only limitations that result in bona fide economic incapacity. A myriad of conditions, not medically diagnosable, can limit productive capacity as much as, and sometimes more than, traditional disability. Domestic violence, shoddy schools, or drug cultures, for example, often limit people's life chances just as much, but just as often they do not come with a doctor's note.

Whatever Americans give through institutional charity and subconscious guilt over hypocrisy, they recoup in resentment and regular opportunities for ostracism. Recipients of social welfare, whose basis is social disadvantage rather than classic incapacity, are viewed with not-so-quiet derision. In the grand scheme of the nation, the American reception of such people is not unlike unwanted pests in a home. To ferret them out, the government places a piece of cheese in a trap then patiently waits. Soon the creatures emerge and partake; upon sight, spectators are reaffirmed of their superiority. An important difference, of course, is that with social welfare recipients the nation's object is eradication through economic rehabilitation rather than through extermination. That the national object is economic rehabilitation, however, does not preclude the interpersonal experience of class indignation and moral disgust.

On the other hand, Americans appear quite moderate or even liberal in their views about economic responsibility when contemplating the socially disadvantaged of other nations. The donation of billions of dollars to lift the citizens of poorer nations seems unattended by the resentment heaved upon the American poor. There are at least three promising explanations for this difference in attitude that are consistent with American conservatism toward economic responsibility. One explanation is that in aiding other nations, Americans are more concerned with humanitarian structural reform—uprooting oppression, promoting capitalism and democracy, stemming pandemic health issues—than with the micro-enforcement of economic responsibility. Another explanation is that, in virtue of the undemocratic and oppressive practices of many of these nations, Americans find little sense in discussing in a serious way those citizens' economic obligations. Yet a third explanation is that much of what Americans know of other countries is obtained from popular news sources, which for the most part are unconcerned with such issues.

OF VOLUNTARY PAUPERS

Turn now to the moral status of paupers in America. Notice that there are only two classes of person capable of provoking the full moral disgust of the American people. The first class of person is unoriginal and historically routine: violent criminals, particularly individuals guilty of sexual offenses. Criminals simultaneously offend the moral, religious, and humanitarian sensibilities, and in equal degree. The second class of person is altogether unexpected: adults who refuse to accept responsibility for their own economic well-being. Where welfare recipients are proved to be voluntary paupers, their booty is ill-gotten; it is a product of misrepresenting their ability to provide for themselves. The existence of many voluntary paupers receiving public assistance would constitute ongoing fraud of massive proportion.

But identifying and counting voluntary paupers is not easy; certainly, there is more to it than Sumner suggests.

Sumner's recommendation that Americans scrutinize the designation "the poor" is wise when interpreted as a warning not to treat the mere fact of economic hardship as proof of some degree of incapacity. I made a similar recommendation in chapter 4 with respect to looking past political designations to the reasons in favor and against particular social courses of action. Once the social designation "the poor" is discarded, however, inquirers accept responsibility for resolving when economic deprivation is the result of free choice and when it is not. Because human beings lack the scientific truth of such ultimate questions, a pragmatic solution is necessary. The pragmatic solution for Americans is to presume the full freedom of persons until presented with irresistible evidence to the contrary.

The American solution explains the sense in which voluntary paupers are free, poor choosers. This way of reaching the conclusion is less metaphysically satisfying than hoped for, though, because it is an approach taken for the sake of convenience rather than in light of the truth of things. This also should make it harder to justify the moral disgust actually visited upon persons designated as voluntary paupers in the United States—though, of course, it does not.

A voluntary pauper is one who, with respect to securing some resource, has it within his power to do more but chooses not to. The most troublesome cases of voluntary pauperism involve people who lack an adequate supply of some important resource, say, food or housing, and for whom the immediate concern is securing an adequate supply. With respect to adequate supplies of food or housing, one is a voluntary pauper for whom basic nutrition and dwelling could be, but for some reason is not, obtained through one's action. These cases are so troublesome because people who lack adequate supplies of important resources often make claims upon the public for support.

It is difficult to distinguish voluntary paupers from individuals who do all they can reasonably be expected to do to fulfill their basic needs. For simplicity's sake, I will call individuals who lack an adequate supply of some important resource but who do all that they can reasonably be expected to do in its pursuit "satisficers." To satisfice is to engage in conduct that, while less than ideal, nonetheless meets a workable standard of human conduct. The term satisficing was first employed by American political scientist Herbert Simon in economic discussions of business decision making.[2] Academic philosophers use a similar concept to discuss practical rationality in relation to whether persons, in seeking what is best for themselves, must always aspire to maximizing or may aspire only to satisficing outcomes. The philosophical notion of satisficing is illustrated by Max Weber's account of traditionalism introduced in chapter 2, where individuals desire wealth only as needed to maintain their economic status quo although greater wealth might yield additional goods.[3]

My use of the concept of satisficing differs from usage in both the economic and the philosophical contexts. Here, it represents the social determination of when, for practical purposes, persons shall be deemed to have met standing social or moral obligations for which perfect compliance is either not feasible or unreasonable. The idea of satisficing amounts of labor is to be contrasted with the virtually unregulated working conditions of an earlier America. Such examples abound but perhaps are best known through Upton Sinclair's *The Jungle*, which described working life in the stockyards of Chicago in the early 1900s, and also from the exploitative practices of manufacturing sweatshops of the same era, which fueled the rise of unions and the enactment of the Fair Labor Standards Act of 1938 (whose purpose was to "eliminate labor conditions detrimental to the maintenance of minimum standards of living necessary for health, efficiency, and the well-being of workers.")

The idea of satisficing is not only necessary for specifying when asking individuals to work more or under less humane conditions, it is also unreasonable. Supposing the existence of adequate working conditions, the concept is also necessary for resolving when the individuals themselves can be said to have fulfilled their work obligations, including obligations they might carry while away from the job. In spite of the Golden Rule's requirement that individuals do their economic best, in an imperfect world we cannot expect individuals to be optimally efficient in their conduct. Individuals will make bad economic choices. They will make waste. Therefore, a standard is needed to evaluate individual work behavior. The notion of satisficing embodies that standard.

The number of hours that a nation determines will comprise the average workweek has a cultural explanation. Assuming that number falls within the range necessary for a society to accomplish its major functions and is not so great or forcible as to constitute injustice, that number is arbitrary from a moral point of view. Once set, however, the number takes on normative significance by serving as one measure for assessing when individuals have met their labor obligations.

First, the codification in law of provisions regulating the socially established workweek, such as mandating pay at rates of time and a half for hours worked per week in excess of forty, create legal entitlements that depend upon value judgments regarding what constitutes reasonable amounts of work. Second, whether reasonable or not, where the majority of people actually work the number of hours specified for the average workweek, simple equality demands that others do the same unless there is a good explanation. Thus, the number of hours a nation has determined will comprise the average workweek becomes its moral standard for satisficing amounts of work, and working full-time becomes a prerequisite for citizenship.

The American standard of satisficing explains why the unaffordable nation is defined in part by the inability of many to afford items of decency while working forty hours per week, and also why, in the United States, it is morally repugnant to suppose that individuals should have to work more than a full-time job just to afford such items, even if many must in fact.

As to the subset of Americans who lack adequate supplies of important resources, whether they are voluntary paupers or satisficers is not just crucial, it is the fundamental issue in the debate over social welfare. Satisficing is the *primary condition* for social welfare eligibility in America. To the extent that persons eligible for social welfare can be designated voluntary paupers, the provision of welfare services is both unnecessary and objectionable. Indeed, the chief dissatisfaction with welfare programs is the perception that benefits accrue mainly to voluntary paupers rather than to satisficers.

The requirement of satisficing has implications that are socially far-reaching and morally unpleasant. An immediate implication is that some people should be permitted to starve and to suffer whatever else follows the absence of economic resources, provided that the lack is attributable to the individual's failure to take reasonable steps within his power that would have averted the situation. A broader implication is that as a matter of principle, the United States could not be committed to the eradication of all social disadvantages and inequality, for that would inevitably mean subsidizing voluntary paupers.

Americans have yet to fully grasp the true nature of this public policy concern. To fill this void in moral understanding, I suspect that many Americans gravitate toward the political parties in virtue of their real or attributed stances of social welfare or seek to judge on case-by-case basis by looking to the histories of individual welfare recipients. But neither politics nor history can answer the distinctly moral question of whether social welfare recipients are voluntary paupers or satisficers. Consider each in turn.

THE FAILURE OF POLITICS

Opponents of social welfare are not so because they are ideologically conservative. They are conservative on the issue of social welfare because they have concluded that most welfare recipients are voluntary paupers and that the public-at-large is being forced to transfer portions of their own economic welfare to improve the lives of lower-class crooks. Likewise, proponents of social welfare are not so because they are ideologically liberal. They are liberal as to social welfare because they have concluded that most welfare recipients are satisficers and that within a shared community, satisficing by the disadvantaged can generate moral obligations among the advantaged.

Rarely in the United States are objections to social welfare libertarian in character, that is, the rejection of social welfare on political principle. Instead, those with objections to social welfare lament poor administration and systemic exploitation by individuals who should be ineligible for benefit but are cheating the public-at-large. Complaints about welfare programs tend to emerge in response to conduct by recipients that, in the complainant's estimation, is economically irresponsible: failure to practice birth control or to search diligently for work; refusing to accept low-paying work or not taking education seriously; expending resources on luxurious items or otherwise living beyond their means, and so on. These are not principled objections to the practice of government helping satisficers to regain self-sufficiency. These are practical objections to perceived policy loopholes that result in subsidies to voluntary paupers.

If it were true that most welfare recipients were voluntary paupers, the vast majority of Americans, liberal and conservative, would oppose social welfare. If it were true that most welfare recipients were satisficers, the vast majority of Americans, liberal and conservative, would support social welfare to some degree. Thus, people claiming to be liberal or conservative for the sake of defending one side of the issue, in truth, are deciding the issue based on whether they believe welfare recipients to be voluntary paupers or satisficers. They have made their choice, and politics is merely a question-begging means of advocacy.

THE FAILURE OF HISTORY

Failing politics, perhaps the problem is one of evidence, a matter of discerning which life histories contain the types of experience American social welfare means to offset. Distinguishing voluntary paupers from satisficers in this way would appear to require historical review of individual lives: genetic or environmental precursors to economic dysfunction, a framework for settling when candidates can be attributed with having missed opportunities, what "an opportunity" will mean for policy purposes, extended choice-histories and impact trajectories, and measurement of current effort.

This information will be unavailable in most cases. Even with full historical information and unlimited administrative resources, these inferences could not be drawn with confidence. That is so because "voluntary pauper" and "satisficer" are moral designations. Historic choices and circumstances are valuable only as empirical indicators of moral status. There is no finite set of actions or combination of them that could provide a definitive checklist. And, in any case, complete individual information would reveal every person to have extensive rap sheets of both pauperish and satisficing conduct.

As in other areas of law where truth is too difficult or costly to obtain, the law of social welfare turns to presumptions. Thus, social welfare programs police the boundaries between voluntary paupers and satisficers by conditioning the continued receipt of benefits upon satisficing, as defined by a discrete set of satisficing conduct, such as holding down a job, undergoing vocational training, using welfare benefits as the law specifies, etc. Many social welfare recipients in good standing may be able to do far more to improve their condition than the law demands of them. Provided such conditions are met, however, the law presumes recipients to be doing well enough.

Thus, voluntary paupers are first and foremost creatures of the American moral imagination, created from the necessity of finding pragmatic solutions to ultimately unanswerable questions about the contours of freedom. After that, and for policy purposes, voluntary paupers are wholly free individuals and also poor choosers, for by American lights such persons fail to do all they might to advance their own welfare. Although it should not upset the American moral practice of erring on the side of free choice—of presuming freedom wherever the truth of the matter is grey—it is worth remembering that there are few, if any, pure voluntary paupers walking this earth. Americans should therefore proceed with humility when drawing upon this damning convention in evaluating the conduct of actual human beings, who are forever an amalgam of good and bad choices, good and bad luck, and good and bad justice. Just as certainly true, when it comes to making one's daily bread, far fewer citizens are pure satisficers than is commonly pretended.

OF INVOLUNTARY PAUPERS

Poor, impecunious creatures! The involuntary pauper is convinced that his market worth—and somehow, therefore, his moral worth—is insufficient to demand the wage necessary to afford items of decency.

The involuntary pauper is different from people whose marketable talents are so paltry as to truly make decent earning impossible. The person who seeks charity from an *accurate* perception of his inability to earn items of decency is not an involuntary pauper; he is just poor and optionless as a matter of fact.

Even the optionless poor can exaggerate their economic lack of value, however; and so they suffer the illusion that they are condemned to destitution when, in fact, their skill set could guarantee them unremarkable poverty. But this is a rather benign form of involuntary pauperism. Once items of decency are objectively out of reach, the game has been lost and all that is worth fighting over are scraps. The scourge of involuntary pauperism plagues mainly the poor with options: poor who, with guidance, character, and luck, might reverse their situations and become self-sustaining.

The American ideal of freedom, combined with the assumption that men are born *Homo economicus*, casts involuntary paupers as freaks of nature, monstrosities lacking the chromosome of dignity amid capitalism. Americans believe that desires for economic independence and self-sufficiency are innate and that they needn't be nurtured any more than parents need learn love for their newborns. If desires for economic independence and self-sufficiency are innate, something very wrong must occur in order to produce involuntary paupers. Consistent with their bipolar attitudes toward economic responsibility and social welfare, Americans offer two very different mythologies of how the innate desire for economic freedom is mutilated so as to produce involuntary paupers. One mythology is based on nurture; one mythology is based on nature.

The public mythology—the one needed to justify the practice of social welfare—posits that involuntary paupers are the products of economic wear and tear. Overexposure to the downsides of economy can induce men to accept their lots, shifting their focus from self-improvement to distraction from deprivation. The public mythology honors the assumption that desires for economic independence and self-sufficiency are innate, and hence rarely in need of rejuvenation. It follows from the public mythology that no person is rendered an involuntary pauper unless he or she has experienced extreme, psychologically debilitating economic hardship. On this basis, the public mythology of involuntary paupers recommends a liberal policy of social assistance. According to the public mythology, the very practice of social welfare comes with the quiet admission that economy can sometimes overwhelm people.

The private mythology—the one needed to preserve Americans' view of themselves as radically free—also assumes the innateness of desires for economic independence and self-sufficiency. Rather than name the vagaries of the marketplace as the cause of involuntary pauperism, however, the private mythology names the involuntary paupers themselves. The private mythology posits that there is something genetically wrong with involuntary paupers. Sustained economic hardship may set off the condition, but moral constitution is the true source. According to the private mythology, involuntary paupers suffer a moral birth defect, a predisposition to succumb to economic pressure more easily than commoners, much as some drunks and gamblers may be predisposed toward abusing those forms of amusement.

Like alcohol and gambling addiction, the private mythology of involuntary paupers casts the associated state of mind as vicious.[4] The private mythology of involuntary pauperism could treat the condition as a form of social disability and make involuntary paupers eligible for social security. Americans generally reject the view that conduct can be externally vicious though not freely or fully chosen, however. Wherever confronted with this circumstance, Americans tend to smuggle in responsibility. Although the private mythology suggests that involuntary pauperism is both a vice and a disability, as a matter of public policy it is treated simply as a vice. Construed as ordinary vice, involuntary paupers are deemed ineligible for social welfare.

The soft spot in both mythologies is the assumption that desires for economic independence and self-sufficiency are innate rather than inculcated or taught by society. Those kinds of desire are of marginal import in precapitalist societies and are more likely products of capitalism than the other way around. Another formulation of the assumption supposes that all human beings have innate desires for *security*; it so happens that in capitalist societies, security requires economic self-sufficiency, which in turn fuels desires for economic independence. In that case, the people of capitalist societies should carry deeply ingrained desires for economic independence and self-sufficiency, because those ends are the basic means of security.

Reinterpreting the innateness of desires for economic independence and self-sufficiency in terms of security comes at a steep price, however. The reinterpretation changes the normative policy aims of social welfare programs. If the condition of involuntary pauperism is causally linked to depressed desires for security, then the provision of transitional economic resources and skills training misses the heart of the problem. In that case, the primary aim of social welfare should be to provide a rehabilitative, psychological service designed to establish or restore the basic desire for economic independence.

Desire management is too much to ask of any governmental program; too much to ask, also, of a nation whose people hold fast to beliefs in radical degrees of free choice. We do not have the resources, or very much of the know-how, to make people want what they seem not to want to strive after. Consequently, what involuntary paupers there are, shall, in the United States, suffer the same fates as others classes who suffer ordinary weakness of will. They must find their own way, or die trying, or die not trying.

NOTES

1. The reference is to Ayn Rand, *Atlas Shrugged* (New York: Plume, 1999).

2. See, e.g., H. Simon, "A Behavioral Model of Rational Choice," *Quarterly Journal of Economics* 69 (1955): 99–118, and H. Simon, "Theories of Decision-making in Economics and Behavioral Science," *American Review* 1009 (1959): 253–83.

3. Here, see generally, Michael Slote, "Moderation, Rationality, and Virtue," *Tanner Lectures of Human Values* (1985); M. Byron, ed., *Satisficing and Maximizing: Moral Theorists and Practical Reasons* (Cambridge: Cambridge University Press, 2004); and particularly, Roger Crisp, "Equality, Priority and Compassion," *Ethics* 113 (2003): 745–63, and "Egalitarianism and Compassion," *Ethics* 114 (2003): 119–26.

4. I believe Kant expresses Americans' considered judgment when he says that "A drunken man cannot be held responsible for his drunken acts; he can, however, for his drunkenness." Within the example lies an explanation of why persons who are disabled from work by vicious conduct receive little empathy. "Habit makes an action easy until it at last becomes a necessity," Kant explains. "Such necessity is a result of habit, because it fetters our will, diminishes our responsibility; yet the acts through which the habit was acquired, must be imputed to us." Practically speaking, there is probably no good method or purpose for bringing individuals to task exclusively for having risked, as opposed to causing damage from having succumbed to, addiction, but something like this is occurring when Americans revile addicts. See Immanuel Kant, *Lectures on Ethics* (Indianapolis: Hackett Publishing, 1963), pp. 62–63.

CHAPTER 6
Poor Justice: Injustice and the Golden Rule

Americans expect no less than that each of us will do his or her absolute economic best, every moment of every day, throughout our natural lives. In a cultural milieu that is fond of celebrating the plurality of thought and diversity of perspective, one will be hard-pressed to upset the universality of this Golden Rule. The notion of one's economic best is remarkably broad. It certainly requires devoting one's energy toward some productive economic activity with a regularity and commitment likely to yield economic self-sufficiency. More so, doing one's economic best requires regulating conduct outside of work that can affect the course of personal, economic development.

In principle, and with luck, work shall consume a little more than one-third of the American adult life. It is the remaining two-thirds of life that is dangerous. In that two-thirds of living human beings make choices that are either conducive to or disruptive of economic advancement. On this subject, Voltaire writes that "our labor keeps us from three great evils—boredom, vice, and want."[1] And Benjamin Franklin, writing under his pseudonym, Poor Richard, recounts this story of his visit to an auction:

> I stopped my horse lately, where a great number of people were collected at an auction of merchant's goods. The hour of sale not being come, they were conversing on the badness of the times; and

one of the company called to a plain, clean, old man, with white locks, "pray father Abraham, what think you of the times? Will not those heavy taxes quite ruin the country? How shall we ever be able to pay them? What would you advise us to do?"—Father Abraham stood up, and replied, "If you would have my advice, I will give it you in short; for a word to the wise is enough," as Poor Richard says. They joined in desiring him to speak his mind, and gathering round him, he proceeded as follows: "Friends," say he, "the taxes are indeed very heavy; and if those laid on by the government were the only ones we had to pay, we might more easily discharge them; but we have many others, and much more grievous to some of us. We are taxed twice as much by our idleness, three times as much by our pride, and four times as much by our folly; and from these taxes the commissioners can not ease or deliver us, by allowing an abatement."[2]

Again, a popular adage in the United States counsels human beings to work only to live rather than live to work. Insofar as the Golden Rule requires limiting conduct that hinders one's economic best, the adage is mistaken. In capitalist societies human beings should live to work. That is, within limits, the American morality of labor requires citizens to live in a manner that preserves their ability to work well.

But enforcement of the Golden Rule can conflict with other American values. One area of conflicts is in relation to family. A corollary of the Golden Rule is to live within one's means, to purchase only as one can afford. An ugly truth about the United States is that some citizens, married and unmarried, cannot afford to have children. By "affording" children I mean that the financial profiles of prospective parents indicate the ability to provide a child with the economic support necessary to ensure the child's welfare.

Some parents who have but cannot afford children will never ask for government support, and their children will become normal, contributing members of society. Other parents who have but cannot afford children will seek government support, and their children will inherit their economic frailties. Such outcomes are not morally irrelevant, however, as the breach of the Golden Rule probably occurs at the point of having children with knowledge that one cannot afford them. Again, parents who cannot afford but have children and who knuckle under and do whatever is necessary to pay for their children's welfare are, in that regard, admirable personages. Often that means working more than a full-time job and, correspondingly, the marked absence from a child's upbringing. But even on this account it does not follow that such parents can afford children. Rather, such parents likely trade the capacity to raise children for the capacity to pay for them.

As I envision it, fully 'affording' children requires wages or other resources that permit parents to devote substantial time to raising them. An insidious but practical implication of the Golden Rule is that poor people and a hefty percentage of middle-class wage earners should refrain from having children because they can only manage to pay for children or raise children, but not both. (Or, alternatively, that in the United States caring for dependents should be treated as compensable or at least socially creditable labor[3]—an issue left unexplored here.)

Americans should have conflicting moral reactions to these observations. One the one hand, procreation is believed to be a fundamental human activity. It falls within the penumbra of basic human rights Americans recognize as privacy and is implicated in substantive equality. To some, conditioning the right to procreate upon the capacity to afford it will seem akin to emancipating slaves without education, job skills, or property, or to granting voting rights but hiding voter's booths or threatening violence against those who would use them. Philosophers have long observed that some rights are empty without the ability to exercise them. Other rights are believed so fundamental that to lack the resources needed to exercise them constitutes a human wrong. Whether having children is this kind of right or being unable to afford children is this kind of wrong is an open question, but the moral concern is well-placed.

On the other hand, suppose it is true that having children is a fundamental right everyone should have the resources to exercise and also that the incapacity to afford children is a human wrong. There remains the brute fact that many Americans simply cannot afford children. It seems morally irresponsible for a society to endorse the practice of unaffordable parenting under the banner of human rights. However one proposes to resolve the issue, nothing undoes the fact that conscious unaffordable parenting breaches the Golden Rule.

Usually when important values conflict, some workable compromise is possible. To impressive degrees, I would argue that this has been true in balancing liberty and equality, democracy and capitalism, religion and toleration. I see no realistic compromise between the Golden Rule and the American commitment to family, however. In a world where working a full-time job and controlling one's economic waste were sufficient to sustain a family, this moral side-constraint of the Golden Rule would not arise. Then, doing one's economic best would not call for many Americans to forego building families. In the unaffordable nation, conversely, doing one's economic best requires a substantial portion of Americans to do just that.

This example is meant to provide readers with a sense of the Golden Rule's reach. Readers should not conclude from this illustration that the Golden Rule is always the predominant consideration in making moral decisions in America. As to the issue of unaffordable parenting, for example, at the point of pregnancy still other values—such as preserving life and/or the freedom of prospective parents to choose what is best for themselves—may be overriding. But, from the perspective of the American morality of labor, such misconduct is serious even though the remedies may admittedly be harsher than the offense.

Some will be convinced that the Golden Rule, as it functions amid the unaffordable nation, works as an injustice upon some Americans. As to building families, the injustice consists of the unfair obligation of some to refrain from having children but could also require low-income earners to sacrifice many uniquely human and humanizing activities. Others will describe this reality simply as moral and economic pragmatism. But there is bona fide injustice in the world, and it is worth asking how the Golden Rule applies to those who experience it.

With each passing day, so too passes thousands of injustices—large and small, deliberate, some with malice, some unintended—against a broad and diverse swath of Americans. Acts of injustice often fetter victims' ability to earn through their labor. Remedying discrimination, in particular, should be a priority in capitalist societies because intentionally derailing another's ability to earn and compete on fair terms is an especially egregious and costly act.[4]

Given the historical importance of discrimination in the United States, readers might expect the Golden Rule to offer an enlightened, forward-thinking approach regarding the economic obligations of victims of injustice. To the contrary, the Golden Rule does not recognize discrimination as a special case at all, except insofar as the whole class of victims of discrimination might be more susceptible to voluntary or involuntary pauperism. That is, far from exhibiting concern that victims of discrimination be accommodated or made whole, the Golden Rule's concern is only that such persons continue to meet their labor obligations while seeking remedial or compensatory justice.

The Golden Rule absolutely prohibits milking adversity in order to forestall return to full economic performance. Events of discrimination create unique opportunities for victims to exploit their circumstances to obtain relief from working. To protect against the risk that victims of discrimination will seek more time or resources than is reasonably necessary to recover, the Golden Rule views with cynicism all accountings of economic and emotional harm of discrimination.

In this way, the relationship between victims of discrimination and the public-at-large is comparable to the relationship between employees who suffer work-related injuries and employers anticipating their return to work. Because employees may be receiving benefits from the employer, such as workers' compensation or disability benefits, and employee absences can cause losses in productivity or profits, employers may seek to minimize the risk that injured employees will remain away from work longer than is necessary. The easiest way to do this is to doubt, question, and scrutinize every claim.

Programs of affirmative action receive special scrutiny under the Golden Rule, in the form of a common but rarely articulated objection. The objection suggests that recipients of affirmative action violate the Golden Rule simply by accepting program benefits because the provision of this kind of opportunity cannot occur without also relieving beneficiaries of effort they otherwise would have to expend to achieve the same ends. The objection is a red herring, however, claiming to take issue on the basis of the Golden Rule but in fact taking issue with relieving beneficiaries of affirmative action of certain labor efforts while leaving them upon nonbeneficiaries of affirmative action.

The Golden Rule ceases to be a functional moral rule when people are judged by factors beyond their control. Beneficiaries of affirmative action do not control the laws that govern them as they control whether they will get up and go to work or school each day, and whether they will work to make the most of their personal circumstances. Since the beneficiaries of affirmative action do not choose this aspect of their economic lives, it is unfair to cite the availability of affirmative action as evidence that they are not doing their economic best.

Moreover, the conclusion does not follow: affirmative action can make economic advancement easier for beneficiaries than for those who do not qualify, resulting in beneficiaries expending less effort to achieve comparable success than in a nonaffirmative action world. All that means, however, is that beneficiaries of affirmative action who are doing their economic best will go further in American life than they would in a nonaffirmative action world; not that the availability of affirmative action disables beneficiaries from doing their economic best.

Here is why this particular attack on affirmative action and its beneficiaries is so offensive. If it were true that beneficiaries of affirmative action violate the Golden Rule simply by accepting program benefits, it would be impossible for racial or ethnic minorities and women to honor the Golden Rule no matter how hard they try, solely because of the existence of a social program. The existence of affirmative action would disqualify most everyone but white males from satisficing. Affirmative action may be objectionable on other grounds, such as reverse discrimination, because the programs typically fail to achieve their goals, are unnecessary, or produce more harm than good. But the argument that programs of affirmative action violate the Golden Rule is a non-starter.

On this issue, beneficiaries of affirmative action and children of wealth make strange bedfellows. Each is stereotyped as incapable of doing their economic best due to grants of assistance: the former from public programs designed to remedy discrimination, the latter from private inheritances. It should be obvious that children of wealth are no more responsible for their social positions than are beneficiaries of affirmative action. Children of wealth do not choose their starting points, and inheritance cannot be counted against them when judging their conduct under the Golden Rule.

But although one's starting place is irrelevant to whether one is presently doing his or her economic best, one's starting place is relevant to what one's economic best looks like and also to the incentives one has to achieve it. Other things being equal, and assuming both do their economic best, we expect children of wealth to meet with much greater success than the persons born into economic hardship. This is not just a factor of cash, but also of human and social capital, influence, and opportunity.

For this reason we must presume that the application of the Golden Rule is scaled, with greater moral credit accruing to those who begin from disadvantageous circumstances. It is no surprise that a rich man becomes president. It is truly an event when a poor man does. For these reasons, rich and poor children are equally intimidated about their financial futures but for very different reasons. Poor children are intimidated about their future because there has been no familial evidence that success is possible. Rich children are intimidated because there is too much familial evidence to allow failure. In the *Oxherding Tale*, American scholar and author Charles Johnson writes of a similar phenomenon as to the pasts of blacks and whites in America:

> This feeling in both that the past is threatening: in the Black world a threat because there is no history worth mentioning, only family scenarios of deprivation and bitter struggle—and failure—against slavery, which leads to despair, the dread in later generations that they are the first truly historical members of their clan; and in the White world the past is also a threat, but here because, in many cases, the triumphs of predecessors are suffocating, a legend to live up to, or to reject (with a good deal of guilt), the anxiety that these ghosts watch you at all times, tsk-tsking because you have let them down; a feeling that everything significant has been done, the world is finished.[5]

That Americans are equally suspicious of wealthy children and beneficiaries of affirmative action is telling. It indicates that Americans dislike anyone who actually receives (or is perceived to receive) resources for free, whether or not government is the provider and irrespective of whether beneficiaries are legitimately entitled. I suspect that it is commonplace for Americans to dislike beneficiaries of affirmative action and children of wealth precisely for having to acknowledge their entitlements.

The Golden Rule conjures a vision of toil, of sweat upon the brow in midnight oil. Beneficiaries of aid, familial or governmental, disrupt this image, encouraging the false inference that such people sweat less than others do. This may or may not be true of wealthy children, as there are no familial or environment barriers to which aid is responsive. The case is different for rightful beneficiaries of affirmative action. If discrimination is real then, absent aid, racial and ethnic minorities and women are unjustly required to sweat *more* than do others just to achieve comparable goals.

Americans are justified in monitoring more closely the sweat expended by beneficiaries of affirmative action, however, for dry brows can be construed as wasting public resources. This fact imposes upon beneficiaries of affirmative action an additional, benefits-based burden to do their economic best. That is why, although there is no practical means of enforcing such a procedure, Americans treat beneficiaries of affirmative action as if they had made a declaration under oath, upon penalty of perjury, that:

BEFORE THE WHOLE OF THE UNITED STATES

1. I, _____, represent that I am a victim of historical or continuing discrimination and therefore am eligible for affirmative action.

2. I furthermore swear that while in receipt of affirmative action I shall do my economic best, lest I breach the terms of the benefit.

3. I understand that part of doing my economic best is to accept the benefits of affirmative action only so long as I earnestly need them, as judged by a reasonable person similarly situated.

Signed:_____Dated:_____

NOTES

1. Voltaire, *Candide* (New York: Barnes & Noble Classics), p. 129.
2. Benjamin Franklin, *The Way to Wealth* (Bedford, MA: Applewood Books, 1986), pp. 9–11.
3. For an argument that unpaid dependent-care work, rather than simply traditional employment, should count toward satisfaction of benefits-based obligations, thus perhaps mitigating or substituting for full-time work responsibilities, see Elizabeth Anderson, "Welfare, Work Requirements, and Dependent-Care," *Journal of Applied Philosophy* 21, no. 3 (2004): 243–56.

4. The literature on the economic costs of discrimination is both vast and contentious, and beyond the scope of this chapter. For my purposes, all that need be true is that discrimination is not cost-free, but rather results in substantial economic costs to perpetrators and victims and society-at-large. A good place to begin this literature is with the writings of Nobel laureate economist Gary Becker. See also Thomas Shapiro, *The Hidden Costs of Being African American: How Wealth Perpetuates Inequality* (New York: Oxford University Press, 2004).

5. Charles Johnson, *Oxherding Tale* (New York: Plume, 1995).

CHAPTER 7
Poor Luck: The Inequity of Disability and Other Struggles

According to the United States Department of Labor, there are more than fifty million disabled individuals in the United States, two-thirds of whom suffer severe disability. Of these fifty-odd million, approximately twelve million are working-age adults. Of all working-age people with disabilities (aged eighteen to sixty-four), only three of ten (32 percent) are employed full- or part-time, compared to eight in ten (81 percent) working-age people without disabilities. However, among the disabled unemployed, two out of three would prefer to work.[1]

People with disabilities are commonly viewed as victims of cosmic injustice.[2] A more accessible description is that people with disabilities often face *inequity*. *Injustice* refers to actions and failures to act that infringe upon people's legitimate moral or legal expectations. Refusing to consider a person for employment solely because the person has a disability—and not for any reason related to the job—is arguably both a moral and a legal injustice, because he or she has both moral and legal rights to equal consideration. On this meaning, however, people with disabilities suffer no obvious injustice for that fact, because there is not natural or political right to be born without disabilities, nor could such rights ever be enforced, except perhaps against God.

Inequity, by contrast, refers to differences in social trait or position that result in incongruities in the life prospects of people. Having a disability that makes it more difficult for a person to compete in the marketplace is one such inequity, because the life chances are thereby adversely affected, and, other things being equal, people without disabilities are likely to have a better shot at decent lives. As explained below, inequities can but do not automatically rise to the level of injustice. Therefore, disabled people who allege that the inequities associated with their circumstances are also unjust face a burden of proof.

Similar questions about the inequity-injustice continuum arise with respect to individuals whose hardship results not from physical or cognitive disabilities but rather from structural and environmental ones. Inequities between people of means and poverty, between people of sound and unsound education, between people of familial stability and orphanages, between people who have suffered and who have benefited from discrimination raise just these concerns. When people demand reforms in education or healthcare, or in the criminal justice system—for that matter, in nearly any public institution—it is from the belief that the inequities that confront the institution have crossed over into injustice.

Cases of physical or social disadvantage such as these are among the leading cases of what I have referred to as "poor luck": circumstances that appear to be beyond an individual's control and that also strike us as unleveling the American economic playing field. This we cannot have, as it hardly seems fair to enforce the Golden Rule against people if they cannot be said to have "chosen" their opening circumstances and if their circumstances are likely to leave them playing "catch-up" for much of their lives. I cannot feel as good about the fact that I am richer or smarter than you, if the possibility that we have not been competing on equal terms forever looms over and nags at me.

This chapter examines how the Golden Rule applies to cases of poor luck, with the primary focus upon people with common physical or social disabilities of the kinds just discussed. Again, the results of applying the Golden Rule are counterintuitive. For, while I have shown that Americans are typically quite harsh and unforgiving in their enforcement of the Golden Rule, there is a tendency to take it easy on people with disabilities. The moral "break" that Americans tend to give people with physical disabilities is not grounded in any argument that such people should carry less labor obligations than people without such disabilities, but rather is probably the result of an improper sympathy—a fellow-feeling—that finds undue expression by bending the Golden Rule.

On the other hand, Americans rediscover their vigilance when applying the Golden Rule to people who suffer social disabilities. Even when it is admitted that a person's life chances have been skewed due to bad breaks that would hobble any person, Americans still expect such persons to make the absolute best of their circumstances. Although I suggest that Americans should find that more cases of social disability result in genuine injustice than is popularly believed, I expect the suggestion to fall upon deaf ears.

US employers are legally required to reasonably accommodate employees with a qualified disability who can perform the essential functions of a job. For example, in order to reasonably accommodate an employee who is recently diagnosed with an intellectual disability, such as attention-deficit/hyperactivity disorder or obsessive compulsive disorder, the employer must consider providing the employee with job restructuring, the assignment of a job coach or an assistant, modification of the employee's workstation, time off for treatment, and perhaps a modified work schedule. The Americans with Disabilities Act (ADA) and similar state laws require such efforts by employers before terminating an employee with a disability to ensure that such persons do not lose their jobs solely because they suffer from a disability.

The legal requirement of reasonable accommodation is one kind of affirmative action for disabled persons, because it involves extending unique consideration to a specific class of citizen based on that group's features—and for the express purpose of helping that group to compete and achieve in the workplace. Reasonable accommodation of people with disabilities probably appears less objectionable than popular forms of affirmative action for race and gender minorities. That is so because it seems possible to create competitive advantages for people with disabilities without, at the same time, imposing competitive disadvantages upon people with them.

But there are forms of affirmative action for disabled people that bestow competitive advantages that are possible only at the expense of nondisabled persons. For example, in some cases the Americans with Disabilities Act requires employers to give vacant positions to minimally qualified disabled employees, even though the employer has or could easily identify (or simply prefers to search for) more-qualified candidates. That is, in some cases, an employer's failure to give a less though minimally qualified disabled person a position over a more-qualified nondisabled person violates federal (and often state) law.[3] Until recently, federal law was also unsettled regarding whether the ADA required an employer to give a less though minimally qualified disabled person a vacant position despite the employer's uniform policy of hiring only the best-qualified candidates for any position.[4]

People who object to affirmative action for race and gender minorities because it distributes benefits based on characteristics unrelated to one's ability to perform should experience even greater offense at this kind of affirmative action for disabled people. In most cases, affirmative action for race and gender minorities is legally permissive—institutions may, but are not required to, engage in such practices. On the other hand, these programs of affirmative action for disabled people described above are *legally mandatory*—institutions must sometimes prefer minimally qualified disabled people to better-qualified nondisabled people, even if they would prefer not to. If there is such a thing as reverse discrimination, this is certainly it. Yet there has been little public outcry against this kind of affirmative action for disabled people.[5]

Purportedly, affirmative action is a tool for achieving justice. Furthermore, the argument that affirmative action is reversely discriminatory is a criticism of form—it applies irrespective of whom the particular beneficiaries of affirmative action are. And, if it exists, the injustice is the same whether the benefit of affirmative action accrues to people with dark skin or to people who are palsied or have cancer. Therefore, it makes no sense to complain about the matter of affirmative action for race and gender minorities because it is reversely discriminatory but also to support affirmative action for people with disabilities despite the fact that it is reversely discriminatory.

Is there something about people with disabilities, or alternatively about women and minorities, that explains why bestowing advantages upon one is cause for civil unrest but bestowing advantages upon the other is morally uneventful? One explanation is that confronting physical disabilities causes Americans to suspend moral judgment and to refrain from demanding of disabled people what they aggressively demand of everyone else—that they do their economic best. This habit could be a side effect of using people with disabilities as a paradigm for determining when reductions in economic responsibility are justified. The habit could also be due to ingrained humanitarianism. People with disabilities often face challenges that people without disabilities can readily identify with. The awareness of differences in physical capacity is often poignant when persons without meet persons with disabilities: encounters with the blind can cause one to relish vision; encounters with amputees can momentarily return joy to the mundane activity of walking.[6]

Notwithstanding these moments of compassion, which have their place, it is certain that some people with disabilities are also voluntary paupers: they are out to milk the system. The propensity to treat people with disabilities as categorically less economically responsible may also push disproportionate numbers toward involuntary pauperism. Bending the Golden Rule in this way therefore serves no one, neither people with disabilities nor the rest of us.

The misplaced compassion that I have supposed Americans to sometimes feel for disabled persons may temporarily be turned to our advantage, however. Affirmative action for the disabled brings into relief one important justification for the practice: *economic inclusion*.[7] In debates over affirmative action for race and gender minorities, opponents of the practice are often dismissive of the goal of economic inclusion. But a forceful argument in favor of affirmative action for people with disabilities—of the sort that would require giving disabled employees pride of place over more-qualified, nondisabled candidates—is difficulty of fit.

When people with disabilities already have suitable employment and stable, trusting relationships with their employers and co-workers, it makes sense for the law to seek to preserve those relationships. When a disabled person loses his or her job, the chance that he or she will remain in the workforce is dramatically improved by requiring the employer to find them other suitable work if possible, even if that means passing over more-qualified candidates. Any other practice would erect substantial barriers to disabled people finding employment and remaining employed.

Still, if there is such a thing as reverse discrimination, this is it. But is it not understandable? Is it not worth it? People who object to affirmative action for race and gender minorities on the grounds that it is reversely discriminatory might yet find that the public's interest in affirmative action for people with disabilities outweighs their private interest in avoiding the incremental harms it may cause. If that is the case, however, then they should extend race and gender minorities the same moral courtesy.

Does this make affirmative action for race and gender minorities more palatable? Does it make affirmative action for disabled persons less palatable? These observations do not mean to rob disabled persons of affirmative action or, conversely, to preserve affirmative action for race and gender minorities. Their only purpose is to uncover Americans' attitudes toward the obligations of people with disabilities to do their economic best. The recommendation is that Americans try harder not to transform people with disabilities into the super-disabled by pretending that they are more limited than is the case. Such practices violate the Golden Rule.

Other Americans are free of physical disabilities, but they have not received what most Americans would consider fair chances to obtain the skills needed to earn items of decency through their labor. As explained earlier, these people's lives are notable for the absence, in their years, of adequate support from family, schools, health practitioners, mentors, employers, and so on. The default assumption is that these hardships are merely inequities, not injustices. However, in many large pockets of the United States—most urban centers, in fact—the degrees of these hardships are so substantial that they arguably rise to the level of injustice. A review of socioeconomic circumstances of people languishing in Detroit, Baltimore, St. Louis, New Orleans, Newark, Washington, DC, to name a few cities, speak for themselves on this issue.

The American ideal of economic justice aims to put every person in a position to achieve not material equality but, rather, material *stability* through their labor. In capitalist societies, this is possible only for individuals who possess talents capable of garnering livable wages in the open market, talents whose development normally requires an initial threshold of economic opportunity. Birth into a decimated structure of economic opportunity is arguably an injustice in a capitalist democracy because it disqualifies people from earning items of decency through their labor. This is economic incapacitation—the equivalent of lobotomizing individuals, through a process that permanently severs the connection between these people and the economic nerve centers of the nation. It is no wonder that such people often are reduced to industrial morons.

Even so, the issue before us is whether people who suffer these social disabilities are, therefore, entitled to an adjustment in their labor obligations. That is, does the Golden Rule find special favor with such people in light of their circumstances? It is for social justice reform and the political process to redress the harms of social disability, for future generations at least. Under the Golden Rule, however, the unjust narrowing of economic options does not mitigate the duty to diligently following paths that remain open, as far as a person is able, toward a self-sufficient life. If not college, then a trade school or vocational program; maybe a small business or other entrepreneurial undertaking; or a second job to supplement the inadequacy of full-time wages; failing these, then the armed services; failing that, perhaps marrying well.

Where social disabilities so destroy a person's economic options that affordability with labor is wholly out of range, such persons become legitimate paupers and therefore legitimately become wards of the welfare state. But granting these people a political right to work less than full-time is beyond the pale. According to the American morality of labor, there is no possible injustice that could justify allowing an able mind and body to sit idle, nor that could warrant letting capable human beings lie unproductive by the grace of the state. The Golden Rule exists to keep productive those who are capable of production. Remedial justice must be found elsewhere.

NOTES

1. National Organization on Disability, Harris Survey of Americans with Disabilities (2000).

2. Thomas Sowell, *The Quest for Cosmic Justice* (New York: Free Press, 1999).

3. See, e.g., *US Airways, Inc. v. Barnett*, 535 U.S. 391, 397: "The [American with Disabilities] Act specifies, namely, that preferences will sometimes prove necessary to achieve the Act's basic equal opportunity goal. The Act requires preferences in the form of 'reasonable accommodations' that are needed for those with disabilities to obtain the *same* workplace opportunities that those without disabilities automatically enjoy. By definition any special 'accommodation' requires the employer to treat an employee with a disability differently, *i.e.*, preferentially. And the fact that the difference in treatment violates an employer's disability-neutral rule cannot by itself place the accommodation beyond the Act's potential reach.... The simple fact that an

accommodation would provide a 'preference'—in the sense that it would permit the worker with a disability to violate a rule that others must obey—cannot, *in and of itself*, automatically show that the accommodation is not 'reasonable.'"

4. See, e.g., *Smith v. Midland Brake, Inc.*, 180 F.3d 1154 (10th Cir. 1999); *Aka v. Washington Hospital Center*, 156 F.3d 1284 (D.C. Cir. 1998); *EEOC v. Humiston-Keeling, Inc.*, 227 F.3d 1024 (7th Cir. 2000).

5. Although, an influential study found that about 20 percent of persons interviewed expressed indignation at the special treatment that the disabled receive. National Organization on Disability, Harris Survey of Public Attitudes toward People with Disabilities (1991), as cited in Michael Ashley Stein, "Employing People with Disabilities," in *Employment, Disability, and the Americans with Disabilities Act: Issues in Law, Public Policy and Research*, ed. David Blanck, 56 (Boston: Northeastern University Press, 2000).

6. Here, see Douglas Baynton, "Bodies and Environments: The Cultural Construction of Disability," in *Employment, Disability, and the Americans with Disabilities Act: Issues in Law, Public Policy and Research*, ed. David Blanck, 387–411 (Boston: Northeastern University Press, 2000).

7. *US Airways, Inc. v. Barnett*, 535 U.S. at 401: "The [ADA] seeks to diminish or to eliminate the stereotypical thought processes, the thoughtless actions, and the hostile reactions that far too often bar those with disabilities from participating fully in the Nation's life, including the workplace. These objectives demand unprejudiced thought and reasonable responsive reaction on the part of employers and fellow workers alike. They will sometimes require affirmative conduct to promote entry of disabled people into the workforce."

PART 3
THE COVENANT ON AFFORDABILITY

Introduction:
Labor-Based Entitlements

I magine a society in which individuals carry deep social obligations to work: to make daily, positive contributions toward the satisfaction of existing and anticipated communal needs upon threat of moral exile, but with no assurances or guarantees from government that doing so will curry favor, protection, or insurance when factors beyond individual control result in unaffordability of the basic goods all of us are working for. The slacker and the hard worker receive equal treatment, although one works little or not at all and the other works consistently for an entire lifetime. And although the costs of living undercut the decent purposes for which the society claims to exist, government finds no injustice or necessity for reform, nor a sense of duty toward laborers. Government continues to demand they satisfy the Golden Rule at any cost, even though unaffordability with labor is the predictable outcome.

Unilateral obligations to work are inconsistent with the idea of political community. Moral servitude of this kind is inconsistent with the idea of democratic government. The last three chapters reviewed

143

in great detail the austere labor obligations that every American carries. Meeting those duties is neither unconditional nor a purely private undertaking. Rather, citizens accept the duties to full-time work *in exchange* for government's assurance that full-time work and wages will enable them to afford items of decency. That is, Americans willingly accept the duties of full-time work from the recognition that such labors are necessary to the creation of an affordable nation—not so that they can be crushed under the weight of their own productivity.

The right to an affordable nation and the duties under the Golden Rule constitute a covenant—a Covenant on Affordability—between the American government and its people. That covenant provides that the reward for meeting established labor expectations is wages or equivalent resources that are sufficient to afford items of decency, whatever the going rate for such items is at the time. The Covenant on Affordability explains and validates Americans' outrage at the unaffordable nation. The reality is a breach of social contract.

Chapter 8 provides alternative bases for grounding the Covenant on Affordability, both of which are rooted in the Christian-American value of industriousness. The social contract theory of John Locke has particular relevance here, because his reliance upon the value of industriousness as a basis of both divine and political entitlement is the key innovation needed to explain the American Covenant on Affordability. The theory accounts for the existence, in liberal democracies of a religious cultural bent, of parallel divine and political orders in which God and government are the guardians of their respective realms. Within these parallel orders, the deities issue commands that, if adhered to, give rise to guarantees of security against the dangers of wilderness, both political and divine.

The Covenant on Affordability presumes the political duty to work to (more or less) the end of satisfying socially accepted labor standards. Therefore, the Covenant on Affordability directly conflicts with the libertarian self-image that Americans romantically endorse. Within the libertarian ideal there is no mechanism for shifting the burdens of labor obligations between individuals and the institutions regulating them. Where markets fail in the libertarian state, leaving satisficing individuals unable to afford items of decency, it is an unfortunate but politically unfixable occurrence. That political arrangement translates into a duty of satisficing that expands and contracts with an individual's circumstances. At times the duty of satisficing may be exceptionally light, and at other times, crushingly oppressive.

The libertarian view of labor obligations is at times physical reality, as evidenced by the fact that many Americans must work more than one full-time job to afford items of decency. The emotional attraction to simple libertarianism is nowhere to be found, however, when hardworking Americans fail even though they are doing their economic best. Rather, Americans believe that one function of just political institutions is to protect them against this possibility. Explaining how, in American society, personal industry can create obligations on the part of government gives legs to this American conviction.

I do not rely upon Locke's views to defend the American Covenant on Affordability, however. I allege it to exist in the hearts and minds of contemporary Americans. This route to the Covenant on Affordability begins with the observation that nearly every American sets the minimum value of his or her own full-time labor at the going rate of items of decency.

Chapter 9 expands on the Covenant on Affordability by applying the doctrine to the issues of corporate responsibility, trade, and immigration. These issues have special importance because they concern how the Covenant on Affordability resolves questions about the economic rights of people in the United States other than typical American employees.

Large corporations are fundamental to the Covenant on Affordability for three reasons. First, large corporations are the major employers in the United States. Second, based on their real or perceived earnings, large corporations (and their owners) are expected to underwrite the Covenant on Affordability. Third, globalization has enabled many large corporations to avoid some of the labor costs associated with American economic justice by relocating these costs to less democratic, but still capitalist nations elsewhere.

Trade and immigration are fundamental because they raise the issue of how the Covenant on Affordability applies to foreign individuals and those employed by overseas corporations, many of whom wish to become American citizens or somehow take advantage of economic opportunities in the United States. The status of legal and illegal immigrants before the Covenant on Affordability, and whether such persons have a basis for alleging rights under it, speaks to how open the American Covenant on Affordability is. At the same time, asking whether resident immigrants should receive equal consideration under the Covenant on Affordability will be one factor in establishing economic feasibility determinations. This will force Americans to make judgments about how, for example, the facts of oppression in Cuba or Iran should influence American immigration policy.

CHAPTER 8
The Covenant on Affordability

Once abolish the God, and the government becomes the God.
—G. K. Chesterton, *Christendom in Dublin*

W here is this Covenant on Affordability? At what convention was it ratified, and who were its signatories? Americans think formalistically about their rights. When confronted with a proposed new right or privilege, Americans' knee-jerk reaction is to consult the Constitution and search for the express language. When no such language exists, these good Constitutionalists will politely inform suffragists of the error and be on their way, convinced that they have taken rights seriously.

Americans' legal positivism—the view that the only law there is, is law as it is written down—is short lived, however. Each new generation of Americans is surprised to learn that many of their most cherished freedoms lack reference in the Constitution and, rather, are products, not uncommonly fiats, of statutory law. Furthermore, when Americans are confronted with the fact that some right that they consider to be fundamental is not expressed in state or federal law, rather than renounce the right in accordance with their doctrine, they renounce their doctrine in order to preserve the right. This is true, for example, of the American right to education, which has no reference in the Constitution and which the US Supreme Court had held is not a fundamental right. Americans continue to believe that a quality basic education is a birthright.

The experience of feeling deeply that certain things should be rights and are worth fighting for as rights, even when government says that they are not, introduces Americans to the possibility of uncodified political commitments, commitments that are entrenched in American culture even though they are not fully spelled out or explained in law. The Covenant on Affordability is this kind of political commitment. Its roots are decidedly Christian-American, a political outgrowth of the biblical teaching that "one reaps as one sows."[1] Under the teaching, among other things, the diligent and industrious will be rewarded with good lives, while the inattentive and slothful will suffer:

> I passed by the field of one who was lazy, by the vineyard of a stupid person; and see, it was all overgrown with thorns; the ground was covered with nettles, and its stone wall was broken down. Then I saw and considered it; I looked and received instruction. A little sleep, a little slumber, a little folding of the hands to rest, and poverty will come upon you like a robber, and want, like an armed warrior.[2]

"Reap what you sow" has secular and divine interpretations. The secular reading merely proclaims that hard work pays off. That reading takes no positive view of how the hardworking are to secure items of decency in the face of poor luck and poor justice, but only warns that poor choice results in hardship. The secular reading of "reap what you sow" captures much of Americans' thinking about economic responsibility, poor choice, and paupers. However, it does not explain how Americans moved from the biblical exhortation of industriousness to the expectation that their industriousness will earn them God's assurance of affordability.

To most Americans, "reap what you sow" is a divine proclamation. This reading warns followers that, in the physical world, slothfulness and poverty go hand in hand. But the divine reading of "reap what you sow" also highlights the metaphysical rewards of living according to God's will. On this view, the person who works hard will be provided for: industriousness is a virtue that God rewards with bounty. In this world, the good person does not have to worry about poor luck or poor justice. Whenever those vagrants prevent industrious people from earning items of decency, God's part of the bargain kicks in and provides as needed.

The divine version of "reap what you sow" is a bargain. Followers commit themselves to industry in order to please God, who, in exchange, assures them against the harsh realities of the physical world.

How did government become liable for the Covenant on Affordability? A political account of the Covenant on Affordability can be extrapolated from John Locke's *Second Treatise of Civil Government*, whose account of property rights identifies the Christian value of industriousness as a source of political entitlement:

> God gave the world to men in common; but since he gave it to them for their benefit, and the greatest conveniences of life they were capable to draw from it, it cannot be supposed he meant it should always remain common and uncultivated. He gave it to the use of the industrious and rational, (and labour was to be his title to it); not to the fancy or covetousness of the quarrelsome and contentious.[3]

Locke believed that there are natural limitations on people's rights to exclude others from their property. Among those limitations was that enough other property and property that is as good as what others already hold be left for other industrious people to enjoy. Locke's limitations on property were intended to ensure that every industrious person had access to resources of the quality and the quantity necessary to meet his or her basic needs. According to Locke, every industrious person has such natural rights because God gave the world to them—the industrious—in common. So, for Locke, the industrious were entitled to the resources sufficient to meet their basic needs, and it was their labor that created the entitlement.

Locke began with the assumption of bountifulness in nature. He assumed that enough quality resources existed in nature to meet the needs of all the industrious, provided each respected the natural limits on property that he proposed. With the introduction of money, however, Locke was confident that the prohibitions on hoarding property could be done away with. Then, industrious people could work for wages and buy the things they needed with the money they earned through their labor. Locke predicted that this new arrangement would result in huge inequalities between people, but he assumed that was all right because everyone had agreed to use money in the first place.

As others have observed, this argument assumes that by consenting to a transaction, one thereby consents to any and every consequence that could possibly follow, which is false. But I am more interested in the effect of this turn of events on the right of industrious people to have enough and as good of resources. In order to preserve those rights in a market economy, the industrious must be able to afford the price of basic goods with the wages they earn through their labor. A nation in which the industrious are not able afford the price of basic goods with the money they earn from working would arguably violate its citizens' natural property rights.

So, it is possible to locate in Locke's theory of property a requirement of affordability—for the industrious, at least. In order for government to protect citizens' natural rights to property, then, it is obligated to keep life affordable for the industrious. This interpretation of Locke supposes that he requires the redistribution of wealth when doing so is necessary to ensure that all of a society's industrious members can afford items of decency through their labor.

This is all that the average American needs to know about Locke: as I read him, he means to say that industrious Americans are entitled to an affordable nation, and, where necessary, government is required to act to make an affordable nation possible. In order to properly close this discussion of Locke, however, for students of philosophy, it is necessary to say a little more about his theory.

Locke had an interesting view of how individuals come to own "things." In short, he believed that a person gains a property interest in a thing by mixing his or her labor with it. A house is yours because you build it; an apple that falls from a tree belongs to you at the point you pick it up, and so on. For Locke, the reason that such actions gave rise to ownership interests is because the investment of labor is what gives things value in the first place. Locke's view of how people come to own things must be found awkward today, where most people receive only wages in return for their labor and rarely gain ownership interests in the things that they help to produce. Nonetheless, additional support for my reading of Locke is that it fits neatly with his labor-mixing theory of creating value.

Mixing one's labor with things in Locke's state of nature creates ownership interests that are carefully tailored both to the human need for which labor is undertaken and to the amounts of labor expended. By contrast, labor in a market economy yields only what the market determines the labor to be worth. For the most part, market economies do not consider the human needs that motivate people to work or the significance of the amounts of labor that people devote to working. Thus, in moving from Locke's state of nature to civil society, a natural proportionality is lost between the labor people undertake to meet their basic needs and the guaranteed returns on labor investments.

In Locke's natural world, basic goods are so plentiful that people can simply leave their homes and immediately dig into earth to satisfy their needs. In such circumstances, the duty of each person to leave enough good property for others is satisfied mainly by the fact that they are all in the Garden of Eden—a place of virtually unlimited resources—than the fact that people consciously limit their property accumulation to fulfilling basic needs. Put another way, in Locke's state of nature, guaranteeing industrious people basic goods in exchange for work should be understood as a unilateral contract, because God has already discharged his obligation to create bountiful nature. In civil society, on the other hand, where resources are often scarce and subject to market conditions, the duty to ensure that the industrious have enough good property falls to government. This is the Lockean route to the Covenant on Affordability.

We do not need Locke to prove the existence of the Covenant on

Affordability in the United States. If Americans were asked to place a value on their full-time labor, nearly everyone would respond that his or her labor is at least worth the wages necessary to afford items of decency. Indeed, Americans reject the possibility that the value of their full-time work could ever fall below the going rate of decent lives.

This observation is important because it reveals a kind of consensus among Americans in support of the Covenant on Affordability. Each citizen believes that government is obliged to create an affordable nation *for him or her* in virtue of the full-time work that they contribute. No one disputes that some full-time work is *worth more* than the going rate of items of decency, especially when divisions of labor are factored in. But Americans' belief that full-time labor is minimally worth decent lives seems occupation-independent. That is, for the most part, Americans believe in decent wages for full-time work, regardless of the type of work that an individual performs.

POOR MAN'S HEAVEN OR RICH MAN'S HELL

Begin with a poor but industrious person. In virtue of her poverty, something like a Covenant on Affordability is always at the front of her thoughts. For her, the sting of unaffordability is, too, the sting of an unjust political order. "What more can I do?" is her constant plea to God and government. However she means it, the content of the plea cannot be exclusive or privileged, but it is applicable to all. That is, the logic of her complaint is not simply that it is unjust for only her, to be unable to afford items of decency through her labor, but that it is unjust for *any person*, herself included, to be unable to afford items of decency through labor. Thus, whatever this woman's account of justice, it would be underserved by creating affordability only in her case. Justice would require making life affordable for every person who labors as she does.

Then she receives an economic turn of fortune, moving her up to the middle class: a promotion, a winning lottery ticket, an inheritance, a lawsuit, a crime. The stability of her new economic circumstances leaves her less attuned to any covenant, less zealous about its enforcement, more insensitive to people still in financial straights. Thoughts of the industrious poor may briefly cause her to reminisce, only to be extinguished by a sumptuous meal, the many distractions of disposable income, or the pride (and exhaustion) of maintaining a home. After some time, she is little more than an armchair advocate—a person willing to support the cause of affordability, provided she is asked for only her blessing and never her feet.

Some years later, the woman has a bright idea and strikes it rich. What of any Covenant on Affordability now? *Things have changed.* Our rags-to-riches woman has had time to do some mythmaking. Her memory of herself in times of unaffordability with labor has been romanticized. Now it is a grand saga of bootstrapping—of how people can overcome unaffordability through effort if only they are dedicated, meaning that truly there is no such thing as unaffordability with labor. She has also glorified the chain of events leading to her prosperity. In such events, there was no luck, only wise choice. Now talk of a Covenant on Affordability makes her suspicious—and resentful, because now she is among the class expected to underwrite the Covenant with her capital.

Turn now to a person born into wealth. From his perch, the belief in the Covenant on Affordability is heresy. Even before having the chance to prove his mettle in the marketplace, he knows this much: his inheritance and the luxuries he is accustomed to must be protected. Discontent to live in the shadows of his ancestors, he sets out to make his own way. "Making his own way," of course, includes making the most of his inheritance, exemplary education, political connections, and so forth, all of which gives him a better starting position than other men to start empire-building. This man leaves his home each morning fully convinced that only the cream rises, and also that if he becomes independently wealthy, the only possible cause is his own industry. He probably even fantasizes that, if not careful, he could be bested by some poor genius.

Then he receives an economic turn of misfortune and descends to the middle class. Suddenly, there is a direct connection between the things he owns and the wages he earns for the amount of labor he gives. He is forced to trade downward: the mansion for a more modest home; the Rolls-Royce for a Subaru; for his children, an Ivy League school for a state university. For the first time, he notices the exorbitant costs of basic things like health insurance and daycare, which causes in him an entirely new feeling—sticker shock. He presses on, though. His pedigree has granted him an indelible confidence about his ability in the marketplace. But even so, his labor has a new character. In richer times, the failure to get up and go to work was merely a personal failing that could be cured the next day. Now it means risking items of decency. This man cannot help but feel some depression due to these new burdens. Having not been raised under them, he lacks the subtle immunities that poorer men have built up.

Then an event happens: a car is lost, a relative is hospitalized, or maybe a spouse is downsized. Over the next few months, creditors for basic things go unpaid and some of those basic things move into the category of "unaffordable." Still gallant about his market value, his own experience of unaffordability with labor must mean that many others are in his same position. He thinks to himself that he is—no, *we are*—doing what is expected of us in terms of labor, but the returns are not enough to live on decently. What does he do next? The only thing he can do. He complains to God and government, "What more can I do?" He is using all his powers to make his way in the nation. His last, best hope is clemency from those gods powerful enough to intervene on his behalf—gods authorized to manipulate the oppressive factors of the economy that are beyond his purview. He has laid the philosophical foundations of the Covenant on Affordability.

Our rags-to-riches woman and riches-to-rags man each value the Covenant on Affordability according to their economic circumstances. The richer they are, the less valid the Covenant on Affordability is to them. The poorer they are, the more valid the Covenant on Affordability is to them. This raises the concern, discussed in the introduction to the book, that the working person's demand for better wages and benefits really has no foundation, but that it is merely a product of hardship. That is, that the moral valuation of labor, which supposes that people who work full-time are entitled to the going rate of decent lives, is less about justice than about the willingness of the economically disadvantaged to say whatever is necessary to get ahead. If poor people reject the Covenant on Affordability as soon as they become economically successful, the doctrine itself appears to be a political ploy.

But things may also be viewed from the other side. Perhaps the problem is not with poor people trying to enforce, but is rather with rich people trying to avoid the enforcement of, the Covenant on Affordability. That is, in the hands of rich people, perhaps the economic valuation of labor is being overstated and being used as a excuse not to support decent lives in exchange for hard work even though that is what rich people want for themselves. If, as suggested above, rich people are quick to embrace the Covenant on Affordability as soon as they fall upon hard times, then maybe the doctrine is valid after all, and the political campaign of some rich people to disclaim it is less about justice than about shirking their own civic responsibilities.

In any case, what I have tried to show above is that the Covenant on Affordability is the *Poor Man's Heaven and the Rich Man's Hell.* The question for Americans is, which view is the better one for the United States? If we side with the Poor Man, we will embrace the Covenant on Affordability for all and try to explain to rich people who disclaim it that the policy is also there for them should they meet with hard times, provided that they are hardworking. If we side with the Rich Man, we will reject the Covenant on Affordability for any and try to explain to poor people that it is unfair to expect society to share responsibility for them, even if they are hardworking.

One way of summarizing the argument of *The Unaffordable Nation* is that this America should be the Poor Man's Heaven. As argued throughout, America should not be heaven for just any poor person, but only for poor men and women who are failing even though they are doing their economic best. An inevitable consequence of making America this kind of Poor Man's Heaven, however, is that it will seem to some wealthy Americans to also be the Rich Man's Hell. But again, America should not be hell for just any rich person, but only for rich men and women who refuse to accept any share of responsibility for ensuring that every American is able to obtain items of decency through his or her labor. Even in the Rich Man's Hell, rich men and women get to keep a great deal of their property and will receive exceptional wages and benefits for their exceptional skills and industry (or inheritance).

This is the sum of American laborer's position: American workers claim both political and divine rights to an affordable nation. Through their full-time labor, they satisfy their economic obligations to government and God, shifting the burden to each to protect them from the wilderness, that is, to ensure that the rewards of their labor enable them to afford decent lives. To be clear, government and God are jointly and separately liable for keeping America an affordable nation. An unaffordable nation is a breach of contract.

NOTES

1. See Galatians 6: 4–10: "All must test their own work; then that work, rather than their neighbor's work, will become a cause for pride. For all must carry their own loads. . . . Do not be deceived; God is not mocked, for you reap whatever you sow."

2. Proverbs 24: 30–34.

3. John Locke, *Second Treatise of Government* (Indianapolis: Hackett Publishing, 1980), pp. 21–22.

CHAPTER 9
Some Applications: Corporations, Immigration, and Trade

Is the improvement in the circumstances of the lower ranks of the people to be regarded as an advantage or as an inconveniency to the society? The answer seems at first sight abundantly plain. Servants, labourers, and workmen of different kinds, make of the far greater part of every great political society. But what improves the circumstances of the greater part can never be regarded as an inconveniency to the whole. No society can be flourishing and happy, of which the far greater part of the members are poor and miserable. It is but equity besides, that they who feed, clothe, and lodge the whole body of the people, should have such a share of the produce of their own labour as to be themselves tolerably well-fed, clothed, and lodged.
— Adam Smith, *The Wealth of Nations*

OF FALSE GODS: PAGANS AND IDOLATERS OF COMMERCE

The Covenant on Affordability is a contract between government and citizens regarding one political constraint on free markets. In prosperous times, the prerogatives of the Covenant on Affordability lie dormant mostly; then, the claim of corporations to operate unencumbered is the most legitimate. In difficult times, however, the corporation, like other economic institutions, is legitimately called upon to participate in satisfaction of the Covenant.

The limit of private corporations' public responsibilities is an issue that is unresolved in the United States. At one extreme is the view that corporations are private property that is beyond the reach of mandatory civil service. At the other extreme is the view that corporations are a kind of public utility, a highly efficient form of charitable organization whose private ends are subordinate to the common good. I do not believe there is any deep, philosophic truth about which view of corporations is best or most consistent with other American values. As noted in the introduction to the book, on this and many other issues there is only what Americans can and cannot live with.

In any case, both views on the public responsibilities of private corporations are mistaken and inconsistent with the Covenant on Affordability, as well. I believe these unhealthy attitudes toward corporations stem from certain psychoses—literally, losses of contact with reality—on the subject of capitalism. The belief that corporations may be treated like public utilities has much to do with a primitive hostility toward commerce, and also with the association of corporations with everything that is bad about American society. The belief that corporations have no public responsibilities has to do with primitive idolatry of commerce, and the association of corporations with everything that is right American society. Through the filtered lens of either extreme, however, the corporation is transformed from what it is—one kind of legal ownership sensitive to the will of the community—into a religious icon.

There are many Americans who condemn large corporations—not particular ones whom they suspect of misconduct, but large corporations in general. The sentiments are odd, to say the least. It would similarly be odd to resent limited liability companies, or seek to ban general partnerships, or to distrust any sole proprietors on general principle. These Americans are probably suspicious that "S" and "C" corporations are actually code for "Scylla" and "Charybdis." In Greek mythology, Scylla and Charybdis were sea monsters on either side of a narrow strait of water, and in moving away from one, seafarers would inevitably move toward the other. In similar fashion, Americans hostile toward corporations in general seem to feel that their dangers are unavoidable. In fact, the corporation, the limited liability company, the partnership, the sole proprietorship, and other business forms are merely types of legal ownership. They have no moral status apart from their ability to capture and carry forward people's rights.

I suspect that the hostility of many Americans toward corporations is actually hostility toward commerce itself, which shares much in common with making sausage. Commerce is not for the feint of heart. It is understandable that Americans who cherish kind and gentle societies take umbrage with the gladiatorial habits of business people. Still, the American child raised to believe that the United States' means of production is immoral is pushed toward a vow of poverty for all the wrong reasons.

Many thinkers, such as Thoreau discussed earlier, have published moral concerns about capitalism, such as how the demands of business decrease the freedom for humanizing activities:

> The world is a place of business. What an infinite bustle! I am awaked almost every night by the panting of the locomotive. It interrupts my dreams. There is no Sabbath. It would be glorious to see mankind at leisure for once. It is nothing but work, work, work. I cannot easily buy a blank-book to write thoughts in; they are commonly ruled for dollars and cents. An Irishman, seeing me making a minute in the fields, took it for granted that I was calculating my wages. If a man was tossed out of a window when an infant, and so made a cripple for life, or scared out of his wits by the Indians, it is regretted chiefly because he was thus incapacitated—for business! I think that there is nothing, not even crime, more opposed to poetry, to philosophy, ay, to life itself, than this incessant business.[1]

Whatever the merits of this kind of observation, it probably takes too much for granted the fundamental freedoms that capitalism makes possible or enhances. Also, this point of view makes light of how difficult human life is without access to *good things*. This is not the glorification of materialism, but it is only the realization that modern human health and well-being requires efficient, mass production—of vaccines, textbooks, clothing, transportation services, computers, food, and much, much else. Americans who believe that the United States would be better off without the corporation, or with less corporate activity, have forgotten their Looney Tunes. Remember the Roadrunner, forever pursued by Mr. Wile E. Coyote? Mr. Coyote had the most remarkable gadgets at his disposal (not even James Bond could do better). Mr. Coyote obtained all of his devices from a company, one company, in fact: the ACME company. Business school students learn early on the importance of the acronym ACME—it stands for *A Company Makes Everything*.

Usually, it is people hostile toward commerce who see few limits on the public responsibilities that government can impose upon corporations. Like people who support the taxation of inextinguishable vices, such as prostitution and drug use, these pagans of commerce believe that if corporations cannot be conquered and capitalism cannot be tamed, then government should seize the revenue streams of these industries for the public good. This belief cannot be justified by the Covenant on Affordability, which requires that the owners of corporations play a limited role in maintaining an affordable nation but that they must otherwise be left to enjoy their property.

Many other Americans are corporate apologists, people who talk about corporations as if they were divine institutions that are somehow exempt from the projects of democratic community. These Americans idolize corporations, likening them to Staffs of Moses and likening government to the Pharaoh of Egypt. As a form of legal ownership, corporations promote the economic freedom of all of us. But these idolaters of commerce carry the notion too far, concluding that placing any limits upon corporations is a kind of oppression. In the minds of these Americans, corporations cease to be mere property arrangements that are open to reconception by the American society that created them. Instead, corporations are viewed as godly arrangements that must remain untouched and that are beyond moral revision.

The theocratic view of corporations endorsed by idolaters of commerce is not supported by the Covenant on Affordability. Modern corporations benefit remarkably from federal and state governments; they are absolutely beholden to them. For example, if not bailed out every few years by using liberal corporate bankruptcy laws, there are entire industries—for example, the American airline industry, and increasingly, the auto industry—that would have crumbled long ago. Americans who are against the socialization of healthcare seem unconcerned over what is essentially the partial socialization of these other industries.

Often, corporate bailouts are good business and good for American society. They enable failing businesses to restructure rather than go insolvent, thus promoting employment. But it is beyond dispute that these privileges are public benefits to the advantage of corporations. For this and other reasons, there is nothing about corporations that excuses them from sharing public responsibility for the welfare of the United States, including by giving effect to the Covenant on Affordability.

Understanding where the pagans and the idolaters of commerce go wrong is useful guidance when trying to strike a balance regarding the public responsibilities of private corporations. Both camps resist burdens imposed by the Covenant on Affordability. Pagans of commerce resist the fact that substantial material inequality is a permanent feature of American life, and they improperly treat the wealth generated by large corporations as an opportunity for major redistribution. The Covenant on Affordability does not support redistribution for any and all purposes, however, but only for ensuring that everyone is able to afford items of decency through their labor. Idolaters of commerce, on the other hand, resist the fact that wealthy individual and corporate persons will always carry disproportionate burdens in support of the Covenant on Affordability. This probably means progressive taxation, but also taking measures to stabilize labor rewards that affect corporations, such as mandating minimum wages in markets that would otherwise pay much less.[2]

Most Americans are probably neither pagans nor idolaters of commerce, in that they have not taken the time to develop a principled view of the matter. Rather, I suspect that most Americans simply follow their moral intuitions about the public responsibilities of private corporations. These people probably only confront the issue piecemeal, such as when considering the fairness of specific public policies (e.g., school funding, restructuring social security, minimum wage laws) and who should pay for them. On issues like these, large corporations are permanent elephants in the room. Because American debates over *how to pay* for social services like education and healthcare quickly devolve into discussions over *who has the ability to pay*, it is understandable that demands for new, or better, or more social services give corporate Americans pause.

Debates concerning funding social services are generally over the heads of most Americans, the author included. But the least Americans can do in considering the fairness of how economic burdens are distributed in the United States is to stay true to their guts. They can, for example, remain sensitive to their own ideas of when their own taxes become excessive, and they can compare their own tax burdens to those of corporations. They can also admit that the argument that some people should pay for the welfare of others simply because they can afford it is probably not a very strong justification for making them do so. My sense is that these small courtesies of public debate routinely are lost, precisely because they make it a little harder to look to private corporations when Americans want something.

Furthermore, most American corporations are not very large. Most of them have few, if any, employees, and they boast revenues that would not even raise an eyebrow. The many, many small corporations in America likely suffer from public perception that corporate giants the likes of Wal-Mart and Microsoft are typical. Using the mega-multinational corporation as the measure for all corporations probably makes it easier to pretend that no one's interests are harmed, or harmed only insignificantly, by the demands that Americans make upon them. Unprincipled demands upon corporations, large or small, are disrespectful of their owners and indefensible under the Covenant on Affordability, because making such demands treats the work aspirations of employees as more fundamental than the work aspirations of employers. There is no such inequality of interests under the Covenant, however, only different duties depending on one's economic position.

I would not hold out hope that Americans will ever become so morally considerate of corporations, especially very large ones. But perhaps if Americans passed through the corporate looking glass and asked what public burdens they would willing accept if they were in an owner's shoes, Americans would move closer to a balanced view of things.

The Covenant on Affordability takes what appear to be fundamental political disagreements over the redistributive functions of American government and reduces them to very ordinary, technical questions of public administration. Much of what I have argued to this point has been to show that Americans actually do believe in the principle of decent lives in exchange for hard work. They are just upset over how publicly expensive it has become to honor that principle.

In fulfilling the Covenant on Affordability, liberals and conservatives, and Republicans and Democrats, may prefer different strategies. Indeed, because they serve only subsets of the American public, the political parties may actually seek to disown parts of the Covenant to spare their constituents the associated costs. That is, we should expect America's political parties to advocate for only the aspects of the Covenant that are most favorable to their constituencies.

The relationship of our political parties to the Covenant on Affordability is not that different than the relationship of American attorneys to the pursuit of legal justice. The American system of law presumes that justice is a by-product of competent advocacy by the lawyers on each side of the dispute. American law trusts that if each side presents its best case, the conclusions reached by a neutral jury will approximate justice. Therefore, American lawyers pursue the personal desires of their clients, subject to the limp ethical restrictions that the American culture of law imposes. In similar fashion, whether and how the Covenant on Affordability is supported is dependent upon the power of American political parties.

THE MORALITY OF TRADE

Although empirical facts cannot change moral principles, they can require that we revise the everyday moral rules that govern us. For example, assuming that capital punishment is permissible, humanitarianism requires that we use lethal injection rather than the electric chair, the electric chair rather than the gas chamber, the gas chamber rather than the guillotine, the guillotine rather than the firing squad (or the other way around), the guillotine or the firing squad rather than hanging, hanging rather quartering, quartering rather than stoning, and stoning rather than the rack. People were justified in using the crasser killing technologies while they were the best available, but they were required to abandon them and to adopt (or to invent) more humane methods when those became available. Just as new developments in killing technology can require revising the moral rules of capital punishment, changes in the ways that the market functions can require revising the moral rules of business, whether local, national, or international.

As should be expected, the fact of economic globalization has caused revisions in the moral rules of American business and has led to fundamental revisions of what might be called "the morality of trade." Before broaching this new economic reality in the world, however, Americans need first to appreciate an old moral reality in the United States. What I have in mind may be called "the costs of economic justice."

Economic justice is expensive. Many products would probably cost a lot less than they do now if American employers were not required to pay minimum wages, unemployment insurance taxes, or social security taxes; or to provide workers' compensation coverage; or to limit the number of hours that employees can be required to work in one day; or to pay overtime for the hours that employees work in excess of forty in one week. Many products would probably also cost a lot less than they do if there were no laws against discrimination or laws permitting unions, both of which create rights, and therefore lawsuits, and therefore labor and employment lawyers.

To the extent such measures fall within the protections of the Covenant on Affordability, it follows that the decent-lives-for-hard-work principle imposes a premium upon all economic activity within US borders. The Covenant on Affordability increases the costs of doing business by a rate set by American morality. Perhaps the costs of economic justice were of no concern when markets were smaller and more domestic, and when many nations had yet to embrace capitalism or democracy. Amid a sea of noncapitalist undemocratic countries, each capitalist democracy will stand out as the Atlantis of its region.

The most profitable means of production (for those who own the means of production, at least) is probably not democratic capitalism, however, but probably is *un*democratic capitalism. As described above, in a well-functioning capitalist democracy, domestic producers share the costs of economic justice. The democratic process enables laborers to turn some of their ideas about social justice and fairness into public policies, many of which affect the ways employers are allowed to do business. In undemocratic nations, where laborers lack the means of political reform, producers face much less social justice regulations, and so they pay far less for any social justice that obtains in such societies. Therefore, if returns on economic investments were all that mattered, the best system would be one that allows producers to avoid the costs of economic justice.

If American producers, in particular, wished to avoid the costs of the American Covenant on Affordability, they would need to find other countries to move to; countries that were both undemocratic in the ways described above but which were also capable of efficient mass production. The host countries would need employment laws that allowed American companies to pay mere fractions of what American workers earn and to require longer hours than can be required of Americans workers, and without overtime pay. Host countries would also need laws that allowed citizens to begin working at younger ages than allowed in the United States and that had no set retirement age. Most important, these host countries would be free of unemployment, disability, and health insurance benefits, and they would have a legal system that is much more employer-friendly than America's. Arguably, the savings that American companies could gain from moving their operations to countries like these would be substantial enough to offset the transportation and other administrative costs of calling foreign countries "Home."

This is no fairy tale, of course. China, India, Korea, and many other countries considered "third world" present opportunities for American corporations to free themselves of the burdens of American employment. Right now, these nations can offer to American companies the economic advantage of discounting products at the significant rate of injustice. Globalization of this kind is the new economic reality that calls for restudy of the morality of trade. This development enables American companies to choose to refuse the costs of the American Covenant on Affordability. Until an American-style expansion of civil rights takes hold in such countries and imposes similar costs for economic justice, the United States shall remain at a competitive disadvantage internationally.

Many economists argue that globalization is a good thing for American consumers. As to consumer issues unrelated to the Covenant on Affordability, I have no reason to disagree with them. I believe the appropriate questions, however, are: is globalization a good thing for American *employees*? and what is the impact of globalization on their ability to earn decent lives through their labor?

As concerns them, I am particularly interested in the view that increasing wages and benefits is futile because producers simply pass such employment costs on in the price of their products. Assuming this is generally true, profit margins still matter. The profit margins sought by companies are only partially determined by labor costs. Labor costs factor into the minimum profit that companies must yield in order to remain solvent, as well as into the profit that can be anticipated from success in particular markets. But many American companies appear to earn profits that far exceed any and everything that they invest in their labor force. Nor are increases in prices always, or necessarily, a function of corresponding increases in the cost of labor.

Raising prices to retain "reasonable" profit margins is different than raising price to obtain "extraordinary" profit margins, however a society chooses to define those terms. In the first instance, producers cannot afford to sacrifice much, if any, profit. In the second instance, producers simply prefer not to part with any profit—a common sentiment, I imagine—but could do so yet retain sufficient economic incentives to stay in business. In any case, my point is not that producers should be more considerate in setting the prices of their products. The Covenant on Affordability does not require people who seek exorbitant profits to moderate their desires. It does require them to play their positions under the Covenant, however. Charge as you will, and subsidize the Covenant as called upon.

In a passage in *The Wealth of Nations*, Adam Smith writes: "Our merchants and master-manufacturers complain much of the bad effects of high wages in raising the price, and thereby lessening the sale of their goods both at home and abroad. They say nothing concerning the bad effects of high profits. They are silent with regard to the pernicious effects of their own gains. They complain only of those of other people." The example Smith offers to illustrate his point is informative:

> In reality high profits tend much more to raise the price of work than high wages. If in the linen manufacture, for example, the wages of the

different working people, the flax-dressers, the spinners, the weavers, etc., should, all of them, be advanced two-pence a day; it would be necessary to heighten the price of a piece of linen only by a number of twopences equal to the number of people that had been employed about it, multiplied by the number of days during which they had been so employed. That part of the price of the commodity which resolved itself into wages would, through all the different stages of manufacture, rise only in arithmetical proportion to this rise of wages. But if the profits of all the different employers of those working people should be raised five per cent, that part of the price of the commodity which resolved itself into profit would, through all the different stages of the manufacture, rise in geometrical proportion of this rise of profit. The employer of the flax-dressers would in selling his flax require an additional five per cent upon the whole value of the materials and wages he advanced to his workmen. The employer of the spinners would require an additional five per cent both upon the advanced price of the flax and upon the wages of the spinners. And the employer of the weavers would require a like five per cent both upon the advanced price of the linen yarn and upon the wages of the weavers. In raising the price of commodities the rise of wages operates in the same manner as simple interest does in the accumulation of debt. The rise of profits operates like compound interest.[3]

Smith attributed the economic problems of his day—which are essentially the same as ours—to government interference in free markets. If markets were left at "perfect liberty," Smith reasoned, the problems considered in *The Wealth of Nations* would work themselves out naturally. This chapter began with another belief of Smith's: every society has an obligation to ensure that its hardworking people are able to earn items of decency through their labor, in virtue of the contributions that they make to the community's success.

Contrary to Smith, the American experience suggests that the decent-lives-for-hard-work principle is not compatible with unrestrained markets. Even if it were true that entirely free markets were humane, there is no necessary connection between unfettered free markets and the quality of life that a society decides all of its industrious should enjoy. The American standard of decency is a national choice, and hopefully also a national commitment. Thus, it is something that must be worked at by government rather than left to private companies and vagaries of the marketplace.

Smith would probably agree, however, that the American media's penchant of making employee wages and benefits the singular cause of the unaffordable nation is mistaken. The lack of investigative reporting on the social costs of seeking too much profit—such as efforts by American pharmaceutical companies to prohibit Americans and the US government from purchasing lower cost drugs from foreign producers—probably leaves Americans less informed about economic justice, including about the ideas that comprise the Covenant on Affordability. The lack of such information also makes employer demands for reductions in labor costs appear without rejoinder. If Americans were better educated about costs of seeking too much profit, they might decide that society is better off without some corporations, who arguably move overseas because the raping is better there.

I believe that the United States and American employees have prostrated themselves enough to prevent any loss of legitimate consortium.

REGULATING ECONOMIC ASYLUM

Americans' anxiety over the immigration is a relative concern. When American life is affordable and Americans feel that they and their products are getting fair treatment abroad, they give little thought to the economic impact of immigrants. When American life is unaffordable, on the other hand, and Americans believe they and their products face international discrimination, then the issue of immigration is taken to be a measure of international justice.

For Americans looking to blame someone for America's problems, immigrants are easy targets. Illegal immigrants, especially, lack the resources to contest such allegations. They are often silent, or silenced, and politically invisible. Therefore, before asking how US immigration policy is implicated in the unaffordable nation, it is worth reminding ourselves of the full humanity of immigrants, regardless of their legal status.

In one sense, citizenship is no accident of birth. Very few nations grant citizenship solely on the basis of having been born on national soil. In Japan, for example, citizenship requires being born of two full-blooded Japanese, making it virtually impossible for immigrants ever to gain citizenship in that country. A resident of Japan might produce ten dozen generations of upstanding human beings, who live and die in service to the country, without any of them ever becoming eligible for citizenship. In another sense, citizenship is an accident of birth. No one decides where and when they are born, or the citizenship rules that will prevail at the moment of birth. In this regard, to be born into a favored nation in a favorable age is one of the most fortunate events that could ever happen to a person.

From the period of human creation to our extinction, only a small percent of all humanity will have been so fortunate. The remaining ratio of people will dream of carrying their bloodlines to richer soil. Prospective immigrants should not be blamed for wishing to immigrate to the United States or to other free, industrialized nations. Usually, all of the moral rules that govern Americans push people in oppressive nations in this direction. Self-preservation, familial obligation, religious and political autonomy, free enterprise, the absence of civil war and other social strife, and the power of a nation to prevent war on itself are enticing to people in nations without these things.

At the same time, few people born into these "destination nations" ever leave. And far more people than destination nations want or can accommodate try to come. These facts make immigration a permanent buyer's market. Destination nations have their pick of the litter. Every prospective immigrant has traits that, when applying for entry, are either desirable or undesirable to destination nations. Consequently, prospective immigrants have dual identities. They are people, of course. But in the large scheme of immigration policy, they are also commodities.

Whenever a group is made a commodity for some purpose, there is a risk that their full humanity and interests will be devalued. Prospective immigrants face the devaluation of their interests by the citizens of destination nations, who often only know immigrants as names on pages, pictures on television, and references and statistics in newspaper reports. From the perspective of the unaffordable nation, prospective immigrants might even be equated with additional mouths to feed, and nothing more.

In an unaffordable nation, immigrants of every kind—whether they are seeking political asylum, joining family or wedding a citizen, international students, or highly skilled employees—are viewed only as seeking *economic asylum*, that is, the freedom to work and earn an American quality of life. Then, the prospect of adding even one more person to the country, for any reason, seems like an indecent proposal. From this point of view, prospective immigrants are conceived in the same way ecologists conceive the migration of foreign mammals, birds, or insects. The nation is placed on notice that if even a few gain entry in unmarked crates, they will destroy the entire eco(nomic)-system and ravage the local wildlife. Beware the immigration flu!

Immigration practices that make it harder for American residents to afford items of decency appear, at first glance, to be violations of the Covenant on Affordability. For example, many Americans believe that increases in immigration can result in the displacement of American workers, or the replacement of them with legal or illegal immigrations willing to work for lower wages and benefits. However, there are many circumstances where Americans should support this kind of market activity, such as when immigrants happen to bring highly specialized skills to the United States and also when such persons can help to fill positions in industries with inadequate labor pools of citizens.

Claiming the Covenant on Affordability to be violated whenever an immigrant holds a position that might otherwise have devolved to a citizen suffers from two flaws. First, the claim falsely assumes that the United States is always better off with jobs in the hands of citizens rather than in the hands of resident immigrants. But, as explained above, immigration is necessary to attract new and greater talent, as well as it is an efficient method of addressing certain labor demands. Put another way, immigration is an indispensable tool for becoming an economic power. Second, the claim is xenophobic, making far too much of the distinction between citizens and noncitizens. A practice of allowing immigration but denying to immigrants roughly equal employment opportunities is to legalize second-class citizenship.

The general riding of immigrants probably masks a much narrower, and more legitimate, concern: the *illegal* immigrant. Illegal immigrants are not created equal, however. The international student whose F-1 visa expires is an illegal immigrant, but, rightfully, she is no center of attention. The international spouse who marries only for a K-1 or a K-3 visa is likewise an illegal immigrant, but he does not receive much press. When Americans worry about "illegal immigrants," they are mainly concerned about the subset of immigrants who come into the United States across its southern border. Many of these are illegal immigrants come to occupy the lower ranks of America's service and farm labor industries.

Now we are getting somewhere. I have argued that America's legal immigrants have a place within the Covenant on Affordability. Also, from a policy perspective there are many forgivable illegal immigrants. There are obvious and important differences between technical violations of immigration policy and violations that thwart the goals of immigration entirely. Treating immigrants who accidentally miss renewal deadlines the same as the immigrants who sneak into the country and work illegally is to compare apples to oranges.

I do not mean to suggest immigrants who come illegally via Mexico are rightly objects of moral criticism, though this may be the case. But in that these illegal immigrants deliberately flout American law, and although they do it for understandable reasons, they are not fast friends. Like all illegal immigrants in the United States, those coming from Mexico have rights—costly rights—such as the right to have their children attend public schools.[4] By some estimates, currently there are more than a million children of illegal immigrants attending American public schools. Because the United States grants citizens on the basis of geographic birth, moreover, unlike Japan, in America it is possible for illegal immigrants to birth US citizens.

The above helps to explain why many nations are reluctant to grant citizenship on the basis of geographic birth. Any mass exodus into the United States, by any population, however deserving, would probably violate the Covenant on Affordability. A nation that has determined that every human being in residence upon its soil—legal or illegal—should enjoy certain basic protections risks a strain on those benefits if too many persons gain entry. Here, humanitarianism, as well as civic sensibility, counsels exclusion.

This cool, moral geometry is upset by the fact that many illegal immigrants are already in the United States, however, and are not easily removable. Though related, stopping illegal immigration is a separate issue from what to do with the illegal immigrants who are already here. It is useful here to dispel several poor arguments that commonly arise on this subject.

The first argument supposes that all undocumented immigrants in the United States must be deported because any program of amnesty or of makeshift naturalization would be unfair to those who respect American immigration policies. Whatever independent merit this argument enjoys, it is likely facetiously offered by most Americans, who exhibit as little concern for immigrants applying for residence legally as for immigrants seeking illegal entry. Furthermore, as already explained, immigration is an extreme buyer's market that is subject to the needs and circumstances of destination nations. It would be no special injustice to immigrants taking legal steps to gain entry into the United States if the country were to decide that it was worthwhile to legalize a special class of illegal immigrants. Indeed, I do not think immigrants seeking residency in the United States could object if the US government determined it best to deny categorically entry to all citizens from his or her home country. Those practices may be inequitable, but they would not be unjust.

The second argument claims that any special program designed to legalize resident illegal immigrants is a bad idea because doing so would encourage prospective immigrants around the world to bypass American immigration law, smuggle into the United States, and hold out for the next wave of amnesty. This argument betrays a certain fatalism regarding the prospect of America ever securing the Mexican border. For assuming secure borders, it does not matter that would-be illegal immigrants find inspiration in American programs of amnesty. Furthermore, whatever incentives are created by an amnesty program will be short-lived and are probably quite meager in comparison to the incentives many people have to escape the circumstances of their home countries.

A third argument, this time advanced by supporters of a more liberal immigration solution, reasons that because most illegal immigrants in America are only technical rather than bona fide criminals and also because many of them hold productive jobs and have employers who wish to retain them, such immigrants have somehow *earned* a conditional right to legal status. To start, we should question the claim that such people are not "criminals," if only of the white-collar sort. And Americans now know from experience that white-collar criminals can destroy many more lives than, say, a serial killer, whose reign of terror is limited by physical access to victims. Furthermore, it seems irrelevant that immigrants who have forced their way into the United States have demonstrated their good intentions and are working hard. Were I to show up at your place of work unannounced and begin performing valuable service without your employer's permission, it would be nothing short of extortion to conclude that the employer thereby owes me wages for the services forced upon him. Defenders of this argument often take it one step further, though. Not only must employers compensate such people for the value of the services, they should also give the bad Samaritans permanent, full-time jobs.

Benefit by force in violation of law should not give rise to valid claims, whether to employment or to residency. What does count, though, is the apparent fact that many American employers wish to employ such people. These interests of American employers must be discounted, however, to the extent that their support for illegal immigrants is motivated by the desires to exploit their labor. If the employers currently supporting work visas for illegal immigrants were to learn that such workers planned a mass unionization movement for decent wages, I suspect that the employers' tunes would quickly change.

The Covenant on Affordability takes special notice of every human being on US soil. If human beings are here and cannot be purged, the American way is to provide them with basic rights and privileges and take up their immigration status only after caring for them. At the same time, the Covenant on Affordability should not send the message that anyone who forces passage into the United States and perseveres will ultimately be rewarded with permanent residency. Nor could America's absorption of the gutsiest illegal immigrants control for accomplished humanity. Recall that destination nations seek and have the privilege of accepting only immigrants who can make positive contributions to the country. Many of the illegal immigrants who succeed at getting into the United States are certain to be economic duds. That is, at the time of entry, many illegal immigrants will simply be irredeemable, too far gone to be of much economic use to themselves or to the United States.

The United States has not found a way either to expel or absorb illegal immigrants, but the Covenant on Affordability demands that one or the other be done. It is out of step with the spirit and moral forthrightness of the Covenant on Affordability to cast a blind eye toward millions of illegal immigrants whom Americans know to be here but to allow them to languish just beneath our official lines of vision. To the extent they are a problem, this fact adds valuable context to proposals to grant illegal immigrants legal residency. Admittedly, proposals to legalize resident illegal immigrants are a swipe in the direction of accommodation, and also a muted concession of victory to illegal immigrants themselves. But the proposals are also a nod in the direction of American moral decency. The thought of having to legalize millions of illegal immigrants because of the US government's inability to exclude them rightly causes moral chagrin. But giving the illegal immigrants legal status makes them conditional friends, and imposes upon them all of the economic obligations that US citizens already carry. That move also helps to ensure that all working-age persons on American soil, illegal immigrants included, uphold their part of the Covenant on Affordability. The solution is not pretty and may only be temporary, but it is decent.

As long as America's southern border is insecure, the only effective plan for slowing illegal immigration is to cease granting American citizenship on the basis of geographic birth. Removing geographic birth as a basis for American citizenship would significantly quash any hopes of illegal immigrants of laying legal roots through population. The reason that this alternative has not even been proposed in public debate on immigration, however, is that this solution to the problem promises to harm American citizens far more than illegal immigrants every could. To understand how different the United States would be without geographic birth as a basis for citizenship, Americans need only revisit my observations about Japan discussed earlier.

A less radical proposal recommends cutting off benefits currently afforded to illegal immigrants, such as school eligibility for their children. In my view, Americans are right to cultivate all humanity upon its soil. The lives of human beings are not neutral. Every person in the United States—legal or illegal—will either positively or negatively affect the nation's welfare. Denying basic education and other goods to illegal immigrants will not make them leave, for America could never simulate the hardships of Mexico or Central America. However, these measures will dramatically reduce the chances that illegal immigrants will positively contribute to the nation's well-being. Such messy charity is yet another cost of economic justice in America, mandated under the circumstances by the Covenant on Affordability.

NOTES

1. Henry David Thoreau, "Life without Principle," in *Walden and Other Writings* (Barnes & Noble Books), p. 350.

2. Investors in publicly traded corporations are an interesting case. Individuals who simply hold shares in a corporation wish only for stock prices to rise. Usually, such persons pay no attention to whether the value of the holdings increases due to product innovation or slave labor. Such narrow economic interests encourage the less savory aspects of capitalism, making corporations answerable to an amorphous body whose singular purpose is to profit, partly by cost avoidance. The regulations associated with an unaffordable nation are one species of cost that a rational investor could wish to avoid, though from their positions as ordinary members of the society the same arguments in favor of the Covenant on Affordability apply.

3. Adam Smith, *The Wealth of Nations* (New York: Everyman's Library, 1991), pp. 87–88.

4. Although, as explained earlier, the Supreme Court has held that education is not a fundamental right, the court has also held that it would violate the Equal Protection Clause of the Fourteenth Amendment to deny children access to public schools based upon their immigration status. See *Plyler v. Doe, 457 U.S. 202 (1982)*.

CONCLUSION
Labor as an American Institution

It is not needed nor fitting here that a general argument should be made in favor of popular institutions, but there is one point, with its connections, not so hackneyed as most others, to which I ask a brief attention. It is the effort to place capital on an equal footing with, if not above, labor in the structure of government. . . . Labor is prior to and independent of capital. Capital is only the fruit of labor, and could never have existed if labor had not first existed. Labor is the superior of capital, and deserves much the higher consideration. Capital has its rights, which are as worthy of protection as any other rights. Nor is it denied that there is, and probably always will be, a relation between labor and capital producing mutual benefits. The error is in assuming that the whole labor of community exists within that relation. . . . Many independent men everywhere in these States a few years back in their lives were hired laborers. The prudent, penniless beginner in the world labors for wages awhile, saves a surplus with which to buy tools or land for himself, then labors on his own account another while, and at length hires another new beginner to help him. This is the just and generous and prosperous system which opens the way to all, gives hope to all, and consequent energy and progress and improvement of condition to all. No men living are more worthy to be trusted than those who toil up from poverty; none less inclined to take or touch aught which they have not honestly earned. Let them beware of surrendering a political power which they already possess, and which if surrendered will surely be used to close the door of advancement against such as they and to fix new disabilities and burdens upon them till all of liberty shall be lost.

—Abraham Lincoln, "First Annual Message to Congress,"
December 3, 1861

I have tried to reconstruct the morality of labor of the American people, less in theory than from the daily experiences of the common citizen. The account has been pieced together by listening to the way American citizens reason over their lives: what they hope to accomplish in and with their jobs; the significance of working well and of recognition for doing so; whom they are willing and unwilling to help and under what conditions; their impressions of brethren in economic strata different than their own; their notions of property; the role of government in economic justice, at home and abroad; and, ultimately, what a fair return on a full day's work is. The result is the Covenant on Affordability, which, while finding a home within the heart of every American, is selectively repressed in the political minds of the same.

In closing, I call readers' attention to an excerpt from Abraham Lincoln's "First Annual Message to Congress," delivered December 3, 1861. The excerpt is important because it contains Lincoln's vision of labor, a vision that simultaneously grounds the Covenant on Affordability and legitimates Americans' outrage at the unaffordable nation. That vision consists of four propositions, which taken together comprise an unequivocal rejection of economic optimism as wholly out of step with the American project of freedom. The propositions are that:

- Labor is a political institution;
- Labor is prior to and independent of capital;
- Labor is a form of political participation;
- Labor is a primary source of public hope and motivation.

Labor is a political institution. Economic optimism casts labor as if it is little more than an empirical reality, a primordial trait of human life largely unaffected by politics or the choices that a society makes. That view is false. As Lincoln makes clear, labor is a *political* institution, similar in kind to voting and education, all of which play indispensable roles in ensuring equality of opportunity for all. Like education and voting, labor is also a *popular* institution, for one of its functions is to place all Americans on equal moral footing by positioning each to achieve economic stability (and the dignity and respect that comes with it) through the choice to work hard.

Americans have no difficulty understanding voting and education to be popular political institutions. Americans make this connection with voting through their discontent with the impact of wealth upon the political process and by supporting campaign finance reform to restore the principle of "one person, one vote." Americans make this connection with education through their outrage at the systemic failures of public education to live up to its reputation as the Great Equalizer, especially for inner-city families. Voting and public education are not under any threat to disappear, however. They will always be American institutions. Nonetheless, Americans understand that these institutions can fall into disrepair and can only be brought to perform their true functions through national reforms.

Due, in part, to the misguidance of economic optimism, Americans have lost sight of the fact that labor is also a political institution. As a political institution, labor can fall into disrepair, and is only as healthy as the nation's support for it. The health of labor, like the health of voting and education, is as much a matter of national choice as it is individual choice. As I have argued throughout this book, the good citizen's choice to work hard can mean very, very little if the United States has not made valuing labor a national priority.

Labor is prior to and independent of capital. Lincoln's observation that labor is prior to and independent of capital is not the universal claim that it appears to be. It is not a general philosophical claim about how labor should be valued in relation to capital under ideal circumstances. It is a specific political claim about how labor must be valued in order to advance the particular ideals of the American nation. In his own words, Lincoln's concern is over the attempt by some "to place capital on equal footing with, if not above, labor *in the structure of government*."

To ask what roles of labor and capital play in the structure of American government is to ask what each is *supposed to do* for the nation and its people. On this question, there is much more to say of about labor and capital than that they are the respective inputs and outputs of free markets. If that is the question, then Americans must ask why the United States opted for free markets at all. The reasons were then, and are now, that a free market system is the most promising system of production for meeting the needs of the American people and for Americans to address those needs most directly through their labor.

In Lincoln's view, making capital equal to or greater than labor casts labor as having no fundamental role in the success of the United States. In that case, the primary economic concern of American government would be only that the nation as a whole generates sufficient capital. In that case, too, government would lack principled reasons for looking past labor products to the nature of the labor itself. Similarly, if American government was unconcerned about preserving a moral relation between labor and capital and was only concerned to get the amount of capital it needs, it would not matter whether the source of that capital is American labor or the labor of workers from other nations.

Once labor is understood as an American institution, it becomes evident that labor performs social functions other than maximizing productivity. Labor is prior to and independent of capital in the American structure of government because, like voting and education, it is directly related to the roles that the United States needs its citizens to play. For Lincoln, it is not necessary to link labor to capital to understand this. In fact, part of Lincoln's point is that it is impossible to fully appreciate the institutional role of labor in America if labor is reduced to its market value.

Lincoln's argument that labor is prior to and independent of capital is tantamount to my argument that the moral valuation of labor is indispensable to the well-being of the United States. As conceded in the introduction to this book, the economic valuation of labor has its place, a place sufficiently important to take steps to ensure that American markets remain substantially free. But the economic valuation of labor cannot be the end of the story—or even the start of the story. The need for substantially free markets places important constraints on labor as an American institution. However, that need does not entirely usurp, or even always trump, the other functions that labor must perform in America.

Therefore, irrespective of what is going on in the world, including the impact of globalism upon the morality of trade, the health of the United States requires a moral valuation of labor. That is, the United States must find a way to value labor to preserve it as a political institution, not simply as the fuel of production. This is the sense in which Lincoln considers labor to be prior to, and independent of capital.

Labor is a form of political participation. Yet another oversight of economic optimists is that, in at least two important respects, labor is a form of political participation.

First, citizens who give their pound of flesh through work, law abidance, and paying taxes do not view themselves as engaged in a wholly private enterprise. They link their labors to the success of the nation. Americans do not work simply to earn wages that will allow them to send their children to whatever public schools exist. They also work so that public schools exist in America that they will want to send their children to. Americans understand that worthwhile social services such as public education must be paid for and that the institution of labor—their labor—plays a key role in the quality of institutions they can expect enjoy.

Second, for Americans working hard is at some level an act in defense of the American way of life, much like choosing to vote. It is not enough for Americans to be able to vote. It is also necessary that the institution of voting be effective. Americans would find no pride or solace in voting if the institution itself were shown to fail as a vehicle for representative democracy. That is why Americans are so concerned by the malfunction of (and possible malfeasance by individuals in) voting ballots in recent presidential elections.

Americans measure the efficacy of voting by its ability to ensure that each citizen's vote counts for as much, or as little, as the vote of every other citizen. Americans measure the efficacy of labor as an institution by their ability to live decently by it. This should help to explain why Americans rightly believe the unaffordable nation to be a political issue. Complaints about the unaffordable nation are political objections to the inefficacy of labor as an institution.

The failure of economic optimists to understand labor as a form of political participation leaves them unable even to comprehend the unaffordable nation. In response to Americans' demand for decent lives in exchange for hard work, economic optimists respond, "We cannot afford it." The response is much like telling slaves that the United States cannot set them free because the nation is too economically dependent upon chattel slavery, or like telling citizens who are denied voting rights that the financial investment necessary to make the institution valuable *for all* is cost prohibitive.

Economic optimists miss that *there is no economic justification for political injustice*. Economic optimists can try to convince Americans that justice does not require decent lives in exchange for hard work, but the recitation of statistics will never do. As long as Americans believe the unaffordable nation to be a political injustice, a denial of the right to effective labor, the only solution is restoring the efficacy of labor as an American institution.

※

Labor is a source of public hope and motivation. Finally, labor is a fundamental spring of public hope and individual motivation. As Lincoln observes, the poorest of America's citizens—the prudent, penniless beginners—have absolutely no reason to believe that they can improve their circumstances other than through their labor. Absent that fundamental enticement to working hard, Americans might as well try their luck at lawsuits and lotteries. Americans are not so fickle that they can sustain these positive economic sentiments without seeing a correlation between labor and return.

Working forty hours per week for a mere fraction of a living wage is eroding Americans' hope in their labor. Yet economic optimists dispense with hope altogether. As explained earlier, the desire to obtain items of decency may get a person to work, but increasingly that desire is getting people to *charge*, to delve deeper and deeper into the credit welfare system. And while the desire to obtain items of decency may keep a person working, I sincerely doubt that it is enough to make good employees of people.

Lincoln understood how important it is for Americans to believe that they can succeed by their own labor. Lincoln also understood that such beliefs are not hallucinatory; they cannot be faked, but are the products of economic conditions that make decent lives possible in exchange for hard work. Lincoln, at least, links these positive sentiments to economic growth and innovation, as well as to the characters of Americans. Americans are better for having—and for being able—to succeed by their labor.

"Closing the door on advancement," as the unaffordable nation is doing, is not harmless. I have tried to show that at some point Americans will lose faith in their labor and will turn to other, less savory means of getting a living. Being an industrious people, this is what we should expect them do to. Americans cannot reasonably be expected to waste their industry pursuing dead options simply because those options are moral and legal, or to refrain from pursuing their only live options simply because those options are immoral or illegal.

The operative rule in the unaffordable nation is "get yours." That means the American pursuit of immorality and illegality for economic gain. It also probably signals an end to much good that Americans currently do through volunteerism, charitable donations, and the pursuit of careers from a desire to do public good, rather than just for more money. The social costs of Americans' loss of faith in their labor will be monumental.

Lincoln's vision of labor, which I share, is the response to the misguided ascent of economic optimism in the United States. The vision understands that labor is much more than its market value and is actually to be held in higher moral regard than the capital that it makes possible. Lincoln's vision also reveals that the *effectiveness* of labor— the ability of each person to use his or her labor to earn a decent life— is integral to the American model of political and economic justice. Therefore, labor cannot be sacrificed to capital in the manner that is happening in the United States right now without doing real harm to the nation—and to American freedom.

I will count *The Unaffordable Nation* a success if only it makes clearer the moral grounds upon which struggling Americans object to their economic circumstances. Lincoln's speech is partly concerned with taking a position against African American slavery—"whether it is best that capital shall hire laborers, and thus induce them to work by their own consent, or buy them and drive them to it without their consent." Enslavement is not the only means of devaluing labor to the point of injustice, however. Placing capital above labor, so as to deny individuals the freedom to earn items of decency, has a similar result.

The Covenant on Affordability is real to the citizens of the United States. This social contract captures the role of labor in the American program of freedom. Many, many Americans are doing what the United States expects of them in terms of labor contributions. Having done their parts, they are anxiously awaiting the benefits of their bargain. As we speak, their plea to God and government is "What more can we do?" Having issued their pleas, all they can do is wait. The failure of the United States to respond, or even to take such pleas seriously, is at the nation's own peril.

Bibliography

Ackerman, Bruce, and Anne Alstott. *The Stakeholder Society.* New Haven, CT: Yale University Press, 1999.

Amitabh, Chandra, Shantanu Nundy, and Seth Seabury. "The Growth of Physician Medical Malpractice Payments: Evidence from the National Practitioner Databank." *Health Affairs,* May 2005, http://content.healthaffairs.org/cgi/content/abstract/hlthaff.w5.240 (accessed September 20, 2006).

"An Alabama Lottery: Theft by Consent." Alabama Policy Institute (2002).

Anderson, Elizabeth. "Ethical Assumptions in Economic Theory: Some Lessons from the History of Credit and Bankruptcy." *Ethical Theory and Moral Practice* 7 (2004): 347–60.

———. *Value in Ethics and Economics.* Cambridge, MA: Harvard University Press, 1995.

———. "Welfare, Work Requirements, and Dependent-Care." *Journal of Applied Philosophy* 21, no. 3 (2004): 243–56.

Applebaum, Eileen, Annette Bernhardt, and Richard Murnane, eds. *Low-Wage America: How Employers Are Reshaping Opportunity in the Workplace.* New York: Russell Sage Foundation, 2003.

Bentham, Jeremy. *Defence of Usury: Shewing the Impolicy of the Present Legal Restraints on the Terms of Pecuniary Bargains; In Letters to a Friend to Which Is Added a Letter to Adam Smith, Esq. LL.D.; On the Discouragements Opposed by the Above Restraints to the Progress of Inventive Industry.* London: Payne and Foss, 1818. Online at Library of Economics and Liberty, http://www.econlib.org/LIBRARY/Bentham/bnthUs.html (accessed September 20, 2006).

Bergman, Barbara. "Reducing Inequality: Merit Goods vs. Income Grants." *Dissent Magazine* (2006).

———. "A Swedish-Style Welfare State or Basic Income: Which Should Have Priority?" *Politics & Society* 32, no. 1 (2004): 107–18.

Bernstein, Jared. "Wages Picture: Real Compensation Down as Wage Squeeze Continues." Economic Policy Institute, Jan. 31, 2006, http://www.epi.org/content.cfm/webfeat_econindicators_wages_20060131 (accessed September 20, 2006).

Blanchflower, David, and Richard Freeman, eds. *Youth Employment and Joblessness in Advanced Countries.* Chicago: University of Chicago Press, 2000.

Blanck, David, ed. *Employment, Disability, and the Americans with Disabilities Act: Issues in Law, Public Policy, and Research.* Boston, MA: Northeastern University Press, 2000.

Blum, Lawrence. *"I'm Not a Racist, but ...": The Moral Quandary of Race.* Ithaca, NY: Cornell University Press, 2002.

Boaz, David, ed. *The Libertarian Reader: Classic and Contemporary Writings from Lao-Tzu to Milton Friedman.* New York: Free Press, 1997.

Booza, Jason, Jackie Cutsinger, and George Galster. "Where Did They Go?: The Decline of Middle-Income Neighborhoods in Metropolitan America." Brookings Institution, June 2006, http://www.brook.edu /metro/pubs/20060622_middleclass.htm (accessed September 20, 2006).

Brown, Mark, and Robert Puelz. "The Effect of Legal Rules on the Value of Economic and Noneconomic Damages and the Decision to File." *Journal of Risk and Uncertainty* 18, no. 2 (1999): 189–213.

Byron, Michael, ed. *Satisficing and Maximizing: Moral Theorists and Practical Reasons.* New York: Cambridge University Press, 2004.

Calder, Lendol. *Financing the American Dream: A Cultural History of Consumer Credit.* Princeton, NJ: Princeton University Press, 1999.

Citro, Constance F., and Robert T. Michael. *Measuring Poverty: A New Approach.* Washington, DC: National Academy Press, 1995.

Collins, Chuck, and Felice Yeskel. *Economic Apartheid in America: A Primer on Economic Inequality and Insecurity.* New York: New Press, 2005.

Crisp, Roger. "Egalitarianism and Compassion." *Ethics* 114 (2003): 119–26.

———. "Equality, Priority and Compassion." *Ethics* 113 (2003): 745–63.

Donahue, John J., III, and Peter Siegelman. "The Changing Nature of Employment Discrimination Litigation." *Stanford Law Review* 43 (1991): 983–1034.

———. "The Evolution of Employment Discrimination Law in the 1990s: A Preliminary Investigation," in *The Handbook of Employment Discrimination Research: Rights and Realities,* edited by Laura B. Nelson and Robert L. Nelson, 261–84. The Netherlands: Springer, 2005.

Durkin, Thomas, and Zachariah Jonasson. "An Empirical Evaluation of the Content and Cycle of Financial Reporting: The Case of Consumer Credit." Credit Research Center, working paper 64 (2002).

Ehrenreich, Barbara. *Nickel and Dimed: On (Not) Getting By in America.* New York: Metropolitan Books, 2001.

Franklin, Benjamin. *The Way to Wealth.* Bedford, MA: Applewood Books, 1986.

Galbraith, John Kenneth. *The Affluent Society.* Boston, MA: Houghton Mifflin, 1969.

Gordon, John S. *An Empire of Wealth: The Epic History of American Economic Power.* New York: Harper Perennial, 2004.

Green, Thomas A. "Freedom and Criminal Responsibility in the Age of Pound: An Essay on Criminal Justice." *Michigan Law Review* 93, no. 7 (1995): 1915–2053.

———. *Freedom and Criminal Responsibility in American Legal Thought.* New York: Cambridge University Press, forthcoming.

Hanson, Alicia. "Lotteries and State Fiscal Policy." *Tax Foundation Background Paper* 46 (2004).

Harris, Ian, ed. *Pre-revolutionary Writings/Edmund Burke*. New York: Cambridge University Press, 1993.

Hart, H. L. A. *The Concept of Law*. New York: Oxford University Press, 1961.

Henry J. Kaiser Family Foundation and the Health Research Educational Trust. *Employee Health Benefits: 2005 and 2006 Annual Surveys*.

Hochschild, Jennifer. *Race, Class, and the Soul of the Nation: Facing Up to the American Dream*. Princeton, NJ: Princeton University Press, 1995.

Holmes, Oliver Wendell, Jr. *The Common Law*, edited by Mark D. Howe. Cambridge, MA: Harvard University Press, 1963.

———. "The Path of the Law." *Harvard Law Review* 10, no. 457 (1897).

Johnson, Charles. *Oxherding Tale*. New York: Plume, 1995.

Kant, Immanuel. *Lectures on Ethics*. Indianapolis, IN: Hackett Publishing, 1963.

———. *The Metaphysics of Morals*. New York: Cambridge University Press, 1991.

Leibniz, Gottfried W. *Theodicy: Essays on the Goodness of God, the Freedom of Man, and the Origins of Evil*. Chicago: Open Court, 1988.

Locke, John. *Second Treatise of Government*. Indianapolis: Hackett Publishing, 1980.

Loury, Glenn. *The Anatomy of Racial Inequality*. Cambridge, MA: Harvard University Press, 2003.

Madison, James, Alexander Hamilton, and John Jay. *The Federalist Papers*. New York: Penguin Classics, 1987.

McCrary, Joseph, and Thomas Pavlak. "Who Plays the Georgia Lottery? Results of a Statewide Survey." Public Policy Research Series, Carl Vinson Institute of Government, University of Georgia (2002).

Muller, Jerry, ed. *Conservatism: An Anthology of Social and Political Thought from David Hume to the Present*. Princeton, NJ: Princeton University Press, 1997.

Murphy, Jeffrie G., and Jules L. Coleman. *Philosophy of Law: An Introduction to Jurisprudence*. Boulder, CO: Westview Press, 1990.

Murray, Charles. *What It Means to Be a Libertarian: A Personal Interpretation*. New York: Broadway Books, 1997.

Nathanson, Stephen. *Economic Justice*. Upper Saddle River, NJ: Prentice-Hall, 1998.

National Gambling Impact Study Commission Final Report (1999).

National Organization on Disability, Harris Survey of Americans with Disabilities (2000).

Nelson, Laura B., and Robert L. Nelson, eds. *The Handbook of Employment Discrimination Research: Rights and Realities*. The Netherlands: Springer, 2005.

Nozick, Robert. *Anarchy, State, and Utopia*. New York: Basic Books, 1974.

Pound, Roscoe. *Law and Morals*. Littleton, CO: Rothman, 1987.

Rand, Ayn. *Atlas Shrugged*. New York: Plume, 1999.

Rawls, John. *A Theory of Justice*. Cambridge, MA: Harvard University Press, 1971.

Reiss, Hans, ed. *Kant: Political Writings*. New York: Cambridge University Press, 1970.

Scott, Janny. "Cities Shed Middle Class, and Are Richer and Poorer for It." *New York Times*, July 23, 2006.

Sen, Amartya. *Development as Freedom*. New York: Anchor Books, 1999.

———. *On Ethics & Economics*. Malden, MA: Blackwell Publishing, 1987.

Shapiro, Thomas. *The Hidden Costs of Being African American: How Wealth Perpetuates Inequality*. New York: Oxford University Press, 2004.

Shipler, David. *The Working Poor: Invisible in America*. New York: Vintage Books, 2004.

Simon, Herbert. "A Behavioral Model of Rational Choice." *Quarterly Journal of Economics* 69 (1955): 99–118.

———. "Theories of Decision-Making in Economics and Behavioral Science." *American Review* 1009 (1959): 253–83.

Slote, Michael. "Moderation, Rationality, and Virtue." *Tanner Lectures of Human Values* (1985).

Smith, Adam. *The Wealth of Nations*. New York: Everyman's Library, 1991.

Sowell, Thomas. *The Quest for Cosmic Justice*. New York: Free Press, 1999.

Sullivan, Teresa A., Elizabeth Warren, and Jay Lawrence Westbrook. *The Fragile Middle Class: Americans in Debt*. New Haven, CT: Yale University Press, 2000.

Thoreau, Henry David. *Walden and Other Writings*. New York: Barnes & Noble Books, 1993.

———. *Walden and Resistance to Civil Government*, edited by William Rossi. New York: Norton, 1992.

Trattner, Walter I. *From Poor Law to Welfare State: A History of Social Welfare in America*. New York: Free Press, 1974.

United States Office of the Comptroller of the Currency, Advisory Letter 2004-10 (2004).

Van Parijs, Philippe. "A Basic Income for All." *Boston Review*, October/November, http://bostonreview.net/BR25.5/vanparijs.html.

———. "Why Surfers Should be Fed: The Liberal Case for an Unconditional Basic Income." *Philosophy & Public Affairs* 20, no. 2 (1991): 101–31.

Voltaire. *Candide, or Optimism*. New York: Barnes & Noble Classics, 2003.

von Hayek, Friedrich. *The Constitution of Liberty*. Chicago: University of Chicago Press, 1960.

Waltman, Jerold. *The Politics of the Minimum Wage*. Champaign, IL: University of Illinois Press, 2000.

White, Stuart. *The Civic Minimum: On the Rights and Obligations of Economic Citizenship*. Oxford: Oxford University Press, 2003.

Index

ability to pay, 162

abolition of slavery, 17, 19

accommodation, reasonable
  for the disabled, 135–36
  of immigrants, 176

account management of credit cards, 69

ACME (*A Company Makes Everything*), 160

ADA. *See* Americans with Disabilities Act

adjustable rate mortgages, 66

advanced capitalism, 89, 90

advanced democracy, 89, 90

advancement, closing door on, 185

advertising, 58, 67

advocacy and justice, 163

affirmative action, 128–31, 141n7
  for the disabled, 135–36, 137–38
  for race and gender, 136, 137, 138
  See also discrimination

affluent, gambling as entertainment, 52

Affluent Society, The (Galbraith), 57–58

affordability
  belief that all should afford a decent
    life, 93–94
  Covenant on Affordability, 144–46,
    147–56, 157–58, 160, 161, 164–66,
    171–77, 180, 186–87
  economic affordability, 92, 94
  of having children, 124–25, 126
  of items of decency, 152
  with labor, 39, 140
  and Locke's theory of property, 150
  See also items of decency; unaffordability

affordable nation, 144, 150, 156

See also unaffordable nation

airline industry, 161

Alabama Policy Institute, 51–52

American dream, 20, 35

American Express, 67

Americans
  American culture of responsibility,
    105–10
  American value, 94, 124, 158
  asking Americans to want less, 72
  belief that all should afford a decent
    life, 93–94
  Christian-American roots, 144, 148
  and freedom, 17, 38, 41, 53, 60, 93–94,
    107, 111, 117, 118, 147, 180, 186
  hatred of paupers, 98–99, 103–21
  imposing economic responsibility,
    106–107
  moral disgust of, 99, 110, 111–12
  not believing in worth of own labor, 50
  unwilling to seek assistance, 59–60
  vicious conduct of, 119, 121n4

Americans with Disabilities Act, 135–36,
  140–41nn3,7

American Tort Reform Association, 44

amnesty and immigrants, 173, 174

Anderson, Elizabeth, 62

APR (annual percentage rate) for credit
  cards, 69–70

Arizona, 74n6

Arouet, François-Marie. *See* Voltaire

asylum
  economic asylum, 169–77
  political asylum, 171

Atlas Shrugged (Rand), 120n1
auto industry, 161
average workweek, 113–14

bad faith, 94
"bad" man and the law, 48–49
bad Samaritans, 175
bailouts for corporations, 161
Bank of America, 67
bankruptcies, 72
    bankruptcy laws, 27, 62
    choice in declaring, 73
    corporate bankruptcies, 66, 161
    derision shown to those declaring, 62
    numbers of bankruptcies, 61–62
    US Bankruptcy Code, 62
    US Courts Bankruptcy Statistics, 61
beer and ale, 33–34, 36
benefits packages, 20
Bentham, Jeremy, 64–65, 66–67, 70, 71
"best of all possible worlds," 24–27
biblical citations
    Deuteronomy 23:19, 62
    Galatians 6:4–10, 156n1
    2 Kings 4:1, 63
    Matthew 18:25, 63
    Proverbs 24:30–34, 156n2
billionaire vs. destitute man, 90–91
birth control, 115
birthrate
    increases in, 79
    procreation as a right, 125–26
bootstrapping, 153
bountiful nature, 151
Brookings Institution, 26
Bush, George W., 31n6, 96n3

calculus, 24
Calder, Lendol, 60
Candide, or Optimism (Voltaire), 17, 29–30

capital, labor as independent of, 181–83
capitalism
    advanced capitalism, 89, 90
    balancing with democracy, 39, 89, 126
    capitalist democracy, 23, 165–66
    and corporations, 158–60, 177n2
    and live-to-work philosophy, 124
    moral concerns about, 159–60
    promoting, 110
    regulating and redistributing capital,
        89–90
    and remedying discrimination, 127–28
    undemocratic capitalism, 165–66
    view of minimum wage, 91–92
capital punishment, 164
Catholic Church, 62
"C" corporations, 158
Center for Responsible Lending, 74n9
charity, 90, 104, 118, 186
    institutional charity, 110
    private charity, 41, 59
    social stigma of asking for, 98, 103,
        106–107, 110
Charybdis and Scylla, 158–59
Chase Manhattan, 67
Chesterton, G. K., 42, 48
children
    affording to have, 124–25, 126
    benefiting from welfare, 109
    caring for children as socially creditable
        labor, 125, 131n3
    child labor, 23
    of immigrants, 173
    mortality rates and labor supply, 13
    not having economic responsibility, 109
    procreation as a right, 125–26
    of wealth, 129, 130
China and American corporations, 166
choice
    freedom of, 53, 98, 126

historic choice, 116
individual choice, 37, 44
poor choice, 37–38, 91, 98, 100, 103–21
Christian optimism, 28–29
Christians not charging interest, 62
Citibank, 67
citizens and Covenant on Affordability, 157–58
citizenship
Japan's definition of, 170, 173, 176
US definition of, 173, 176
Civic Minimum: On the Rights and Obligations of Economic Citizenship, The (White), 32n14
Civil Rights Act of 1991, 47
civil society, 151
Clinton, Bill, 11, 12
Clinton, Hillary, 87, 96n1
commerce, 157–64
commercial advertising, 58
communitarianism, 108
compassion, 91, 137–38
compensation
low-compensation, 19–20, 115
relationship to labor, 17
valuation of labor, 17–19, 21–23, 22–23, 50, 145, 151, 152, 183
See also wages
Congress, 62, 93, 96n3
pay raises, 96n1
conservatives, 94–95, 115, 116
Constitution of the US, 147, 177n4
consumer advertising, 67
contractual obligations and credit cards, 67–69
corporations, 145–46, 157–64, 177n2
Covenant on Affordability and, 157, 158, 160, 161, 162–63
finding countries friendly to, 166
hostility toward, 158–60

idolatry of, 160–61
liability for wrongdoing, 42–43
size variations of, 162–63
Covenant on Affordability, 144–46, 147–56
Abraham Lincoln and, 180
basic rights and privileges under, 175
as contract between government and citizens, 157–58
and corporations, 157, 158, 160, 161, 162–63
and illegal immigrants, 175–77
and immigration practices, 171–75
protections of, 164–66
reality of, 186–87
and redistributive function of government, 163
validity of, 152–56
See also affordability
credit card debt, 12
changes in terms, 69–70
credit as a private welfare system, 58–59, 67, 70, 71
credit card marketing, 58, 69, 71–72
credit limits, 69
democratization of credit, 64, 66
disclosure, 60–61, 63, 64–65, 67, 68–69, 70
exploitation vs. disclosure and credit, 60–61
historical reality of, 60
minimum payments on, 63, 68
subprime lending, 63–64, 66, 74n9
used as supplemental income to offset indignity of unaffordability, 58–74
voluntary nature of, 64
See also debt
creditors
conduct of, 60
creditor-debtor relations, 63
source of profit for, 63

creditworthiness, 66
crime as source of money, 153
criminals, 111
   illegal immigrants as, 174
culture of responsibility, 107–10

damage awards, 45, 50
death tax. *See* estate taxes
debt, 12, 57
   blamed on debtor, 61, 62–63
   conduct of debtors, 60
   defaults on, 66
   derision of debtors, 62
   distastefulness of, 60
   mortgages, 66, 73, 74n9
   permanent, 59
   personal debt, 60, 61
   See also credit card debt; paupers
decency, inability to afford items of, 75,
     151, 152
   inability to afford items of decency, 38,
     84, 86, 93
   minimum value of labor to allow, 145
   See also indignity of unaffordability
decent lives, 75–84, 84n1
decent living standard, 12–13, 18–19
   Americans' not believing in worth of
     own labor, 50
   belief in, 93–94
   and decent compensation, 21
   defined by American people, 36
   guaranteeing for everyone, 78–80
   inability to afford items of decency, 38,
     145, 152
   as a measure of a good nation, 75–84
   responsibility for providing, 82–83
   vs. self-sufficiency, 80–82
   what is needed to be able to have, 76–78
   worth sacrifice to obtain, 72
   See also indignity of unaffordability;

items of decency; luxuries; necessity;
   standard of living
decent wage, 12, 29, 152, 175
defaults on debts, 66
Defence of Usury (Bentham), 64–65
democracy
   advanced democracy, 89, 90
   balancing with capitalism, 39, 89, 126
   capitalist democracy, 23, 165–66
   and disparities of wealth, 90–91
   and moral servitude, 143
   promoting, 110
   undemocratic capitalism, 165–66
   view of minimum wage, 92
Democratic Party, 85, 89, 94, 163
democratization of credit, 64, 66
Department of Labor, 133
dependents, caring for, 125, 131n3
deportation of immigrants, 173
deprivation, economic, 105, 111, 118, 130
destination nations for immigrants,
     170–71, 173, 175
destitute man, 98, 118
   compared to billionaire, 90–91
   See also paupers
determination, 53
determinism, 97–101
Deuteronomy 23:19, 62
Development as Freedom (Sen), 27–28
dignity, 38
   and community standing, 58
   dignitary vs. economic harm, 47
   and involuntary paupers, 118
   See also indignity of unaffordability
disabilities, 100–101, 106, 133–41
   disability benefits, 127–28
   disability insurance, 166
   disabled not having economic responsi-
     bility, 109
   involuntary pauperism as a disability, 119

mental disabilities, 100–101, 106, 109
nontraditional disabilities, 110
physical disabilities, 100–101, 109
social disability, 119, 139–40
stereotypes and, 141n7
disadvantaged, working, 27, 88
disclosure and credit cards, 60–61, 63, 64–65, 67, 68–69, 70
Discover (card), 67
discrimination, 48, 130, 131, 134, 165
and the disabled, 136
discrimination lawsuits, 46–47
economic costs of, 132n4
and Golden Rule of Labor, 100
institutional discrimination, 86
international discrimination, 169
by race and gender, 100, 137, 138
remedying, 127–28, 129, 165
reverse discrimination, 129, 136–37, 138
See also affirmative action
disgrace of being poor, 37
disposition, 53
distributive justice, 29
diversity, 123
doctors, compensation for, 20
Dodd, Christopher, 63, 74n9
Donahue, John, 46–47
Durkin, Thomas, 61
dysfunctionality
dysfunctional families, 90
economically dysfunctional people, 82–83

economic affordability, 92, 94
economically dysfunctional people, 82–83
economic asylum, 169–77
economic deprivation, 105, 111, 118, 130
economic efficiency, 28
economic entitlements, 90
economic freedom, 7, 91, 118, 160
economic hardship, 92, 119

economic harm, 47
economic inclusion, 138
economic independence, 59, 118–19, 129
economic irresponsibility, 61–62
economic justice, 21, 28, 84, 90, 106, 108, 139, 169, 177, 180, 186
costs of, 146, 164–66
economic moderation, 72
economic morality, 95
economic obligations, 110
economic opportunities, 35, 139
economic optimism, 25–27, 28–29, 30, 81, 180, 184, 186
economic rehabilitation, 110
economic relief for working disadvantaged, 88
economic responsibility, 59, 60, 61, 62, 73, 82, 97, 106–107, 109
economic valuation of labor, 17–19, 21, 22–23, 50, 145, 183
economy, market, 151
education, 77
funding of, 162, 183
as Great Equalizer, 181
and immigrants, 173, 176–77
vs. law enforcement, 83
not a fundamental right, 147, 177n4
right to, 147
and welfare, 99–100, 115
educators, compensation for, 20
effectiveness of labor, 186
elderly, not having economic responsibility, 109
Emancipation Proclamation, 88
"emotional distress" and lawsuits, 49–50
employer-friendly, 166
employers, lack of obligations, 11
Employment Cost Index, 25
"ending welfare as we know it," 11
entitlement, 21, 108

and children of wealth, 130
economic entitlements, 90
labor-based entitlements, 143–46, 150, 155
legal entitlements, 113–14
political entitlement, 17, 144, 149
social entitlements, 17, 95, 139
entrepreneurs, 20
envy, 21, 30–31n2
equality and liberty, 126
Equal Protection Clause, 177n4
eradication
of poverty, 99
of social disadvantage and inequality, 114
of traditionalism, 71
of welfare programs, 91, 110
Estate Tax and Extension of Tax Relief Act of 2006, 87–88
estate taxes, 87–88
"Examination of a Noble Sentiment, An" (Sumner), 75–84
excessive profits, 167
exclusion and citizenship, 173
exploitation
vs. disclosure and credit, 60–61, 63
of immigrants, 175

fair agreements and credit cards, 67–68
Fair Labor Standards Act (1938), 23, 113
Fair Minimum Wage Act (attempt in 2005), 87
Fair Minimum Wage Act (attempts in 2000 to 2004), 89
families, 81, 93, 124
dysfunctional, 90
family income, 26, 64
taking care of, 18, 19, 20, 126
Federal Reserve, 89
Fielding, Henry, 51

firing of an employee, 49–50
"First Annual Message to Congress" (Lincoln), 179, 180
FleetBoston, 67
food, adequate, 77
foreclosures, 66, 73, 74n9
forty hour workweek, 114
Fourteenth Amendment, 177n4
Fragile Middle Class: Americans in Debt, The (Sullivan, Warren, and Westbrook), 63–64, 66, 67
Franklin, Benjamin, 123–24
freedom, 53, 72, 171
in America, 17, 38, 41, 53, 60, 93–94, 107, 111, 117, 118, 147, 180, 186
of choice, 53, 98, 126
and control of environment, 37
and decent life, 93–94
economic freedom, 7, 91, 118, 160
human freedom, 98, 105–106, 159
individual freedom, 8, 41
and responsibility, 105–106
to work, 171
free enterprise, 170
free markets, 12, 92, 182
determining price of labor, 18
free markets always choose best, 29
frivolous lawsuits, 44, 45, 46
Frontline (TV show), 67–68
full-time work and ability to live decently, 11–12, 18, 19, 22, 25–26, 27, 29, 72, 86, 88, 93–94, 114, 144–45, 152, 155

Galatians 6:4-10, 156n1
Galbraith, John Kenneth, 57–58, 71
gambling, 41, 51–52, 53, 54, 119
See also lotteries
Garden of Eden, 151
general partnerships, 158, 159

geographic birth, 173, 176
"get yours" rule, 186
Gilded Age, The (Twain), 60
globalization, 7, 13, 22, 27, 145, 164, 166, 183
God
  acts of, 90
  and bountiful nature, 151
  "God's perfect plan," 24
  God's will, 148
  and human condition, 29
Golden Rule of Labor, 97–101, 113
  and affirmative action, 128–31
  and Covenant on Affordability, 144–46
  poor justice and, 123–32
  poor luck and, 134–41
"good debt," 62
government
  chief obligation of, 80
  Covenant on Affordability as contract with citizens, 157–58
  necessity of, 55n7
  redistributive function of, 163
  role of labor and capital in, 182
Great Equalizer, education as, 181
gross products, 29

Hanson, Alicia, 55n8
happiness, what is required for, 76–78
hard workers vs. slackers, 143
Hayek, Friedrich von, 30–31n2
healthcare, 77
  and medical malpractice payments, 54n3
  socialization of, 27, 161
health insurance, 166
  employment-based, 26
  unaffordability of, 26
Health Maintenance Organization, 26

higher standard of living, 58–59
high-income neighborhoods, 26
historic choice, 116
HMO. *See* Health Maintenance Organization
Holmes, Oliver Wendell, Jr., 48–49
Homo economicus, 118
hostility
  toward commerce, 158, 159
  toward poor, 11
human freedom, 98, 105–106, 159
humanitarianism, 78, 84, 137, 164, 173
  humanitarian structural reform, 110
  naive humanitarianism, 84
  and prayer, 84n2
  problem of, 79–80, 84n2
Hurricane Katrina, 54n2
Huxley, T. H., 27–28

illegal immigrants, 146, 169–70, 171, 172–75
  amnesty and, 173, 174
  deportation of, 173
  See also immigration
Illustrated London News, 42
immigration, 23, 145, 146, 169–77
  See also illegal immigrants; legal immigrants
inability to afford items of decency, 38, 84, 86, 93, 152
incapacity, 109, 111
inclusion, economic, 138
indebtedness. *See* debt
independence, economic, 119–20
India and American corporations, 166
indignity of unaffordability, 37, 72
  and credit card use, 58–74
  as incentive for lawsuits, 46, 47–48, 52
  as incentive for lottery abuse, 46, 52
  See also items of decency

individual calling, 59
individual choice, 37, 44
individual freedom, 8, 41
individual responsibility, 52–53
industriousness, 85, 104, 144, 148,
    149–50, 151, 185
    industrious poor, 23, 24, 152–53
inequalities, 85, 86
    material inequality, 89, 161
    social inequalities, 85, 100–101
inequity vs. injustice, 133–34, 139
inheritance, 129, 153–54
injustice
    and Golden Rule of Labor, 126
    vs. inequity, 133–34, 139
    legal injustice, 100
    political injustice, 184
    poor justice, 37–38, 91, 98, 99, 101,
        108, 123–32
    social injustice, 85
    and unaffordability, 152
    See also justice
innovation, 177n2
insurance, 77
    and lawsuits, 42–43, 48
interest rate
    ability to raise rate, 68, 69
    adjustable rate mortgages, 66
    APR (annual percentage rate) for credit
        cards, 69–70
    morality of interest rates, 65
    not charged among Christians, 62
    as profit for credit card issuers, 63
    social custom and changes in rate, 65
    state laws setting rate, 74n6
Internal Revenue Code, 87
    See also taxes
international trade, 22
interns, 20–21

inventors, 20
involuntary paupers, 99, 104–105, 117–20
irresponsibility, personal, 85–86
items of decency, 75, 151, 152
    inability to afford items of decency, 38,
        84, 86, 93
    minimum value of labor to allow, 145
    See also indignity of unaffordability

Japan's definition of citizenship, 170, 173,
    176
Jews lending money, 62
Johnson, Charles, 130
Johnson, Lyndon B., 11
Jonasson, Zachariah, 61
judgment-proof people, 49
Jungle, The (Sinclair), 112
justice
    and advocacy, 163
    affirmative action as a tool, 136–37
    cost of, 164–66
    distributive justice, 29
    economic justice, 84, 90, 108, 139, 168
    limiting access to, 43–44
    See also injustice
justification
    economic justification, 184
    moral justification, 25
    social custom as, 65

Kahr, Andrew, 68–69, 71
Kant, Immanuel, 121n4
keeping up with Joneses, 60
2 Kings 4:1, 63
Korea and American corporations, 166

labor
    affordability with labor, 39, 140
    child labor, 23

consuming one-third of life, 123
effectiveness of, 186
as form of political participation, 183–84
Golden Rule of Labor, 97–101, 113, 123–32, 134–41, 144–46
labor as a political institution, 180–81
labor as independent of capital, 181–83
labor-based entitlements, 143–46, 150, 155
morality of, 98, 101, 180, 183
obligation to work, 97–101, 127
price for not working, 97
productivity, 29
significance of individual labor, 95
socially creditable labor, 125, 131n3
as source of public hope and motivation, 185–86
supply exceeding demand, 12–13
unaffordability with labor, 41, 46–47, 49, 51, 52, 85–86, 89, 92, 93, 98, 105, 140, 143, 153–54
valuation of, 17–19, 21–23, 50, 145, 151, 152, 183. *See also* compensation
working more than one job, 145
See also compensation; wages
"Land of Opportunity," 19
law, statutory, 147
law enforcement vs. education, 83
laws of supply and demand, 18, 22
lawsuits, 12, 39, 41, 42–51
discrimination lawsuits, 46–47
frivolous lawsuits, 44, 45, 46
lawsuit abuse, 45
overlitigiousness, 44, 45–46, 50–51
tort reforms, 44, 48, 49, 50
and unemployment rate, 46–47
lawyers, compensation for, 20
laziness, 11
leather shoes, 33, 36

legal entitlements, 113–14
legal immigrants, 146, 171, 172
See also immigration
legal positivism, 147
Leibniz, Gottfried, 24, 29
lending, predatory, 60
liberals, 94–95, 108, 115, 116
libertarians, 108, 144–45
liberty and equality, 126
life histories, 116–17
life span and labor supply, 13
limited liability companies, 158, 159
limits on credit, 69
Lincoln, Abraham, 88, 179
vision of, 180–86
litigation. *See* lawsuits; overlitigiousness
live to work, 124
live within one's means, 124
living wage, 12–13, 185
See also wages
loan sharks, 68
Locke, John, 144, 145, 149–52
lotteries, 12, 39, 41, 51–52, 153
and unemployment rate, 55n8
victim of Hurricane Katrina winning, 54n2
Lottery, The (Fielding), 51
low-compensation
acceptance by welfare recipients, 115
and teenagers, 19–20
See also compensation
low-income and credit card debt, 66
low-income neighborhoods, 26
luck, poor, 37–38, 91, 98, 99, 108, 133–41
luxuries, 33–34, 36, 75

Madison, James, 55n7
malpractice. *See* medical malpractice reform
Malthus, Thomas, 13

"man-over-nature," 54n2

market economy, 150, 151

market mechanisms, 27–28

marketplace, 39

market value, 100

market worth, 117

Marquette National Bank v. First of Omaha Service Corp., 74n6

Marx, Karl, 13

mass production, 160

MasterCard, 67

material inequality, 161

materialism, 160

material stability, 139

Matthew 18:25, 63

medical malpractice reform, 44, 54n3

Melville, Herman, 103, 104

menschenwürdiges Dasein. See decent lives

mental disabilities, 100–101, 106, 109
  See also disabilities

merchandising of credit cards, 58, 71–72

Mexico and immigration from, 172–73, 174, 177

Microsoft, 162

middle class, decline in, 26

Mill, John Stuart, 13, 30–31n2

Miller, George, 87

minimum payments on credit cards, 63, 68

minimum-wage laws, 20, 22, 25–26, 31n6, 86–89, 93, 96nn1,3, 162, 164
  differing views of, 91–92

mining accident in West Virginia, 53–54n1

money, introduction of, 150

moral character and ownership of necessities, 37

morality
  choosing to declare bankruptcy, 73
  economic morality, 95
  of interest rates, 65
  of labor, 98, 101, 180, 183

moral break for those with disabilities, 135

moral concerns about capitalism, 159–60

moral disgust, 111–12

morality of trade, 164, 166

morals-based legislation, 65

moral servitude, 143

moral worth, 117

mortality rates and labor supply, 13

mortgages
  adjustable rate mortgages, 66
  foreclosures, 66, 73, 74n9
  subprime mortgages, 74n9

motivation, labor as source of, 185–86

Nathanson, Stephen, 11–14

nation, unaffordable. *See* unaffordable nation

National Gambling Impact Study Commission, 51

nationalism transcended by humanitarianism, 80

necessaries, 33–34, 36

necessity, 21, 75
  distinguished from nicety, 60
  moral character and ownership of, 37
  necessity of survival, 59

Newton, Isaac, 24

New York Times, 19, 61

NGISC. *See* National Gambling Impact Study Commission

nicety vs. necessity, 60

obligation
  benefits-based obligations, 131n3
  to create bountiful nature, 151
  economic obligations, 110
  for employees, 11
  to not have children, 126
  social obligations, 143

unilateral obligations, 143
    to work, 97–101, 127
Office of the Comptroller of Currency
    (OCC), 69–70
opportunists, 45
opportunity, economic, 35, 139
oppression, uprooting, 110
optimism
    Christian optimism, 28–29
    economic optimism, 25–27, 28–29, 30,
        81, 180, 184, 186
    religious optimism, 29
ostracism, 101, 110
outsourcing, 22
overlitigiousness, 44, 45–46, 50–51
    See also lawsuits
overtime pay, 113–14, 165
ownership, 149–51
    legal ownership, 159, 160–61
Oxherding Tale (Johnson), 130

"Path of the Law, The" (Holmes), 48–49
paupers
    America's hatred of, 98–99, 103–21
    involuntary paupers, 99, 104–105, 117–20
    and satisficers, 116–17
    voluntary paupers, 99, 100, 104–105,
        111–15, 116–17
    See also debt; poor; poverty
personal debt, 60, 61
personal irresponsibilty, 85–86
physical disabilities, 100–101, 109
    See also disabilities
plurality, 123
Point Of Service plan (POS), 26
political asylum, 171
politics
    and Covenant on Affordability, 163–64
    invisibility of illegal immigrants, 170
    labor as a political institution, 180–81

labor as form of political participation,
    183–84
political entitlement, 17, 149
political injustice, 184
political slurs, 94–95
    and social welfare, 115–16
unaffordability as a political problem,
    39, 85–97
unjust political order, 152
poor
    choosing to gamble, 51–52
    deserving poverty, 13, 90, 148
    hostility toward, 11
    industrious poor, 152–53
    moral disgust shown to, 111–12
    optionless poor, 118
    shame and disgrace of, 37, 90, 108
    social designation of, 111
    See also paupers; poverty
poor choice, 37–38, 91, 98, 100, 103–21
poor justice, 37–38, 91, 98, 99, 101, 108,
    123–32
poor luck, 37–38, 91, 98, 99, 108, 133–41
Poor Man's Heaven, 152–56
Poor Man's Pudding (Melville), 103
Poor Richard, 123–24
population growth and labor supply, 13
POS. *See* Point Of Service plan
positivism, legal, 147
poverty
    correlation with gambling, 52
    decline in poverty rates, 11
    eradication of, 99
    full-time workers living in, 25–26
    Johnson's War on Poverty, 11, 12
    poor deserving poverty, 13
    See also paupers; poor
PPO. *See* Preferred Provider Organization
practical rationality, 112
predatory lending, 60

preferentiality, 140–41n3
Preferred Provider Organization, 26
private property, 158
problem
    of humanitarianism, 79–80
    of propagation, 79
    unaffordability as a political problem,
        39, 85–97
procreation as a right, 125–26
productivity, 29, 182
profit margins, 167, 177n2
profligacy, 63
progressive taxation, 23, 161
promotion, 153
propagation, problem of, 79
property
    limitations on, 149–50
    Locke's theory of, 149–51
    natural property rights, 150
    private property, 158
proportionality, rule of, 49
prosperity and valuation of labor, 19
Protestant Ethic and the Spirit of Capi-
        talism, The (Weber), 57
Protestant Reformation, 62
Protestant work ethic. See work ethic
Proverbs 24:30–34, 156n2
public dole, 98–99
    See also welfare programs
public hope, labor as source of, 185–86
public policy, 28–29
public responsibility, 158, 162
Puritan ethos, 71

quality of life, 35, 38

race and gender discrimination, 136, 137,
        138
    See also discrimination

rags-to-riches, 154
Rand, Ayn, 120n1
rationality, practical, 112
Reagan, Ronald, 11
reap as you sow, 148–49
reasonable accommodation, 135–36,
        140–41n3
"reasonable" profits, 167
redistribution
    of capital, 89
    redistributive function of government, 163
    of wealth, 85, 150, 161
regulation
    of capital, 89–90
    preserving economic affordability, 92
rehabilitation, economic, 110
religious optimism, 29
"Repricing of Accounts and Other
        Changes in Credit Terms" (OCC),
        69–70
Republican Party, 85–86, 89, 94, 163
resentment, 106–107, 110
responsibility
    American culture of, 105–10
    culture of responsibility, 107–10
    economic irresponsibility, 61–62
    economic responsibility, 59, 60, 61, 62,
        73, 82, 97, 106–107, 109
    freedom and, 105–106
    individual responsibility, 52–53
    personal irresponsibilty, 85–86
    public responsibility, 158, 162
retirement, 166
reverse discrimination, 129, 136–37, 138
    See also discrimination
rewarding work, 77
Ricardo, David, 13
riches-to-rags, 154
Rich Man's Hell, 152–56

rights
  vs. doctrines, 147
  limitations on, 149
Roadrunner, 160
rule of law, 46
rule of proportionality, 49

satisficers, 112–15, 129, 145
  and voluntary paupers, 116–17
  and welfare, 114, 115
savings, 57, 60
Science and Culture (Huxley), 27–28
"S" corporations, 158
Scylla and Charybdis, 158–59
Second Treatise of Civil Government
  (Locke), 149–52
"Secret History of the Credit Card, The"
  (*Frontline*), 67–68
security, need for, 120
segregation of neighborhoods by income, 26
self-image, 144–45
self-preservation, 170
self-sufficiency
  vs. government assistance, 80–82
  innate nature of, 118–20
self-worth and indignity of unaffordability, 47
Sen, Amartya, 27–28
Senate Banking Committee, 63, 74n9
shame in being poor, 37, 90, 108
shelter, 77
Siegelman, Peter, 46–47
Simon, Herbert, 112–15
Sinclair, Upton, 112
60 Minutes (TV show), 19
skills-building, 99–100
slackers vs. hard workers, 143
slavery, 17, 19, 177n2, 186
Smith, Adam, 13, 33–34, 36, 37, 157, 167–68

snake oil, 66
social contract, 95, 97, 144, 186–87
social costs of inability to afford items of
  decency, 38
social custom, 65
social Darwinism, 39, 75
social disability, 119, 139–40
social entitlements, 17, 95, 139
social inequalities, 85, 100–101
social injustice, 85
social justice, 30–31n2, 165
social obligations, 143
social policy, impact of moral and economic valuation of labor, 22
social security, 119, 162, 165
social welfare, 99–100, 115–16
  and involuntary paupers, 118–19
  See also welfare programs
sole proprietorships, 158, 159
stability, material, 139
stagnating wages, 24, 25
standard of living
  and decent compensation, 21
  decent living standard, 12–13, 18–19,
    21, 36, 38, 50, 72, 75–84, 93–94,
    145, 152
  higher standard of living, 58–59
  necessity and luxury items and living
    standard, 36
Standing with Minimum Wage Earners
  Act of 2006, 87
state lotteries, 51–52
  See also lotteries
statutory law, 147
stigmatization of those receiving welfare,
  107, 108
subprime lending, 63–64, 66, 74n9
  See also credit card debt; mortgages
Sullivan, Teresa A., 63–64

Sumner, William Graham, 39, 75–84,
    84n1, 103–104, 105, 111
superiority of those not receiving charity,
    110
supply and demand, laws of, 18, 22
Supreme Court, 147, 177n4

taxes
    changes in tax codes, 11
    and corporations, 162
    estate taxes, 87
    progressive taxation, 23, 161
    reduction of, 86
    tax benefit programs, 22
    unemployment insurance, 164
technological advances and labor supply,
    13
teenagers and low compensation, 19–20
termination of an employee, 49–50
terms of contract for credit cards, 67–69
"third world" and American corporations,
    166
Thomas, William, 87
Thoreau, Henry David, 15, 72, 73, 159
time and a half for overtime, 113–14
Titius, lending money to, 64–65, 66
"tort of unaffordability," 48
tort reforms, 44, 48, 49, 50
    See also lawsuits
trade, international, 22, 145, 146, 164–69
traditionalism, 57, 58, 71, 112
Twain, Mark, 60

unaffordability, 35–39
    due to individual responsibility, 86
    inability to afford items of decency, 38,
        84, 86, 93
    indignity of, 37, 46, 47–48, 52, 58–74
    items becoming unaffordable, 154

with labor, 41, 46–47, 49, 51, 52, 85–86,
    89, 92, 93, 98, 105, 140, 143, 153–54
    as a political problem, 85–97, 152
    "tort of unaffordability," 48
    See also affordability
unaffordable nation, 39, 95, 126, 177n2
    causes of, 86, 92–93, 94, 114, 169
    closes door on advancement, 185
    and Covenant on Affordability, 144,
        156, 180
    "get yours" rule, 186
    and immigrant policy, 170, 171
    as a political problem, 39, 94, 95, 184
    See also affordable nation
undemocratic capitalism, 165–66
undocumented immigrants. See illegal
    immigrants
unemployment insurance, 164, 166
unemployment rate
    and lawsuits, 46–47
    and lottery sales, 55n8
unilateral obligations, 143
unions, 165
United States
    Constitution, 147, 177n4
    definition of citizenship, 173, 176
    items needed for a decent life, 77–78
    as "Land of Opportunity," 19
US Airways, Inc. v. Barnett, 140–41nn3,7
US Bankruptcy Code, 62
US Courts Bankruptcy Statistics, 61
usury, 60, 66–67

valuation of labor. See compensation;
    wages
Value in Ethics and Economics
    (Anderson), 62
vanity, 63
Vietnam War, 11

Visa (card), 67
visas and immigration, 172
Voltaire, 17, 29–30, 123
voluntary nature
    of credit card debt, 64, 70–71
    of lawsuit abuse, 52
    of lottery abuse, 52
voluntary paupers, 100, 104–105, 111–15
    individual histories determining,
        116–17
    and satisficers, 116–17
    subsidizing of, 114
    See also paupers
voting, importance of, 181, 184

wages
    decent wage, 12, 29, 152, 175
    determinants of, 13
    high wages effecting price, 167–68
    living wage, 12–13, 185
    minimum-wage laws, 20, 22, 25–26,
        31n6, 86–89, 91–92, 93, 96nn1,3,
        162, 164
    overtime pay, 113–14, 165
    stagnation of, 24, 25
    valuation of labor, 17–19, 21–23, 50,
        145, 151, 152, 183
    See also compensation
Walden (Thoreau), 15
Wal-Mart, 162
War on Poverty, 11, 12
Warren, Elizabeth, 63–64, 67–68, 70
wealth
    born into wealth, 153–54
    children of, 129, 130
    controlling flow of, 91
    desire for, 57, 112
    disparities, 90–91

    of offender in lawsuits, 49
    redistribution of, 85, 150, 161
Wealth of Nations, The (Smith), 33–34,
        157, 167–68
Weber, Max, 57, 58, 59, 112
welfare programs, 22, 41, 98–99
    children as beneficiaries, 109
    credit as a private welfare system,
        58–59, 67, 70, 71
    cutbacks in, 11
    dependency on, 82
    "ending welfare as we know it," 11
    eradication of, 99, 110
    individual histories, 116–17
    paupers different from those on, 98
    perceived as undeserved handouts, 11
    public expenditures on, 23
    satisficing as condition for eligibility,
        114
    social welfare, 99–100, 115–16, 118–19
    stigmatization of those receiving, 108
    welfare-deserving, 109
    who should pay, 162
Westbrook, Jay Lawrence, 63–64
West Virginia mining accident, 53–54n1
What Social Classes Owe to Each Other
        (Sumner), 103–104
White, Stuart, 32n14
Wile E. Coyote, 160
wine, 33–34, 36
women, historical assumptions about, 106
work. *See* labor
workers' compensation, 127, 165
work ethic, 11, 59
working disadvantaged, 27, 88
work study, 20–21
work to live, 124
workweek, 113–14